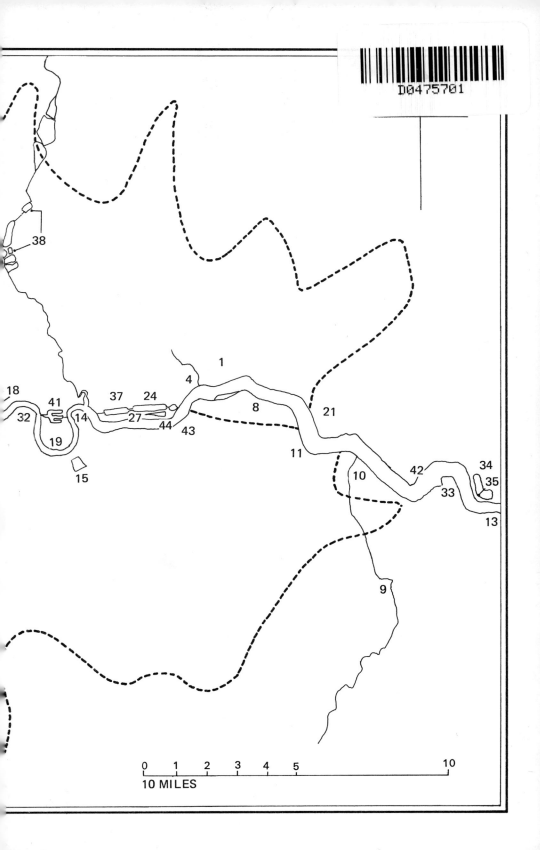

0   1   2   3   4   5   10
10 MILES

THE THAMES TRANSFORMED

00.2

THE THAMES TRANSFORMED

London's River and its Waterfowl

❦

JEFFERY HARRISON
and
PETER GRANT

Photographs by

PAMELA HARRISON

Foreword by

HRH THE PRINCE PHILIP,
DUKE OF EDINBURGH, KG, KT

ANDRE DEUTSCH

First published 1976 by
André Deutsch Limited
105 Great Russell Street, London WC1

Photoset and printed photolitho in Great Britain by
Ebenezer Baylis and Son Limited,
The Trinity Press, Worcester, and London

ISBN 0 233 96840 7

DEDICATED TO
EILEEN GRANT
and to the memory of

CUTHBERT HARRISON
OBE, Legion of Honour

JAMES HARRISON DSC

PAUL HARRISON MM
and

REGINALD HARRISON
OBE, Croix de Guerre,
Legion of Honour, American Bronze Star,

all of whom, through their
association with
J. & C. HARRISON
Ship owners, London,

owe much to the River Thames

CONTENTS

❦

MAPS AND DIAGRAMS

TEXT ILLUSTRATIONS

9

COLOUR ILLUSTRATIONS

BUCKINGHAM PALACE

    For years conservationists have been filling the
air with gloom and despondency. In the laudable attempt
to force public attention to the dreadful things which
mankind is doing to the natural environment there has
been a natural tendency to pick the worst cases.

    Here at last is a success story on such a major
scale that it is worth publishing even at the risk that
it may encourage some people to assume that the problems
of conservation are not really as bad as they were led to
believe.

    The best part about this whole story is the
tremendous encouragement it will give to groups and
organisations all over the world who are struggling
to save the natural environment from largely unintended
destruction. They can all take heart from what has been
achieved in the Thames. The good news is that it can
be done and their schemes too can succeed.

1976.

11

ACKNOWLEDGEMENTS

WE are greatly honoured that his Royal Highness Prince Philip, Duke of Edinburgh, should have consented to write the Foreword for *The Thames Transformed*. As Patron of WAGBI and President of the Wildfowl Trust, there can be no one better qualified to do this. His intense interest in our environment and in the conservation of waterfowl has been a constant inspiration to all those who are involved in these fields.

A great number of individuals and organisations have helped us in gathering together the data for *The Thames Transformed* and we are deeply grateful to them all.

In the Nature Conservancy Council, we express our thanks to Dr P. Gay, Dr B. Green and M. Schofield, successive Regional Officers, S. E. England, and to A. Allison, R. Boston, M. Hudson, M. Labern, E. Pithers, K. Selmes and P. Stuttard. The Ornithological Assessor, A. Colling, kindly arranged collecting licences for our food studies on the Inner Thames.

In the Wildfowl Trust, we are most grateful to Sir Peter and Lady Scott, Professor G. V. T. Matthews, G. Atkinson-Willes, A. St Joseph, T. Bennett and D. Salmon. In particular, the use of the wildfowl count data for Foulness has proved invaluable. Similarly, our thanks are due to Dr J. J. M. Flegg and A. J. Prater of the British Trust for Ornithology, especially for the data provided by the Birds of Estuaries Enquiry which was organised jointly with the Royal Society for the Protection of Birds. Dr L. A. Boorman, of the Institute of Terrestrial Ecology, has helped us greatly with the research projects undertaken over the Maplin developments.

Internationally we have been helped by E. Carp, Dr E. Novak and M. Smart, successive Administrators of the International Waterfowl Research Bureau and we would like to thank Dr W. Erz of West Germany for his help during the Heiligenhaven Conference.

The ready co-operation of the Port of London Authority has been invaluable, especially in our studies on the Inner Thames. We are

ACKNOWLEDGEMENTS

particularly grateful to the Director General, John Lunch; the Director of Tilbury, John Black and N. M. Baker, D. E. Glover, D. Drakley, R. J. Furley, J. R. O'Donnell, J. H. Potter, A. Tetlow and K. Waite for much information and assistance. The PLA has made its launches available to us which has greatly facilitated our regular censuses on the Inner Thames, and we gratefully acknowledge the hospitality extended to us by the crews of the *Benfleet*, *King's Reach*, *Nore*, *Ray* and *Roding*.

The Greater London Council has helped us by allowing access to the Thamesmead site and providing boat transport on the Inner Thames. Our visits to the sewage treatment works at Crossness and Beckton, to the pumping stations and to parts of the sewer system below London have been most instructive. To all those involved we express our thanks, especially Dr P. Matthews who has provided much useful information for which we are most grateful.

The Thames Water Authority, which has been responsible for pollution control in the Thames since its formation in April 1974, has been most helpful. We have had the pleasure of travelling on its new biological research boat *Thameswater*, and we are especially grateful to M. Andrews for providing information on *Tubifex* worms in the river. Mr and Mrs A. Cockburn, formerly with the GLC, have shown a keen interest in our work and have been the source of much technical information about many aspects of pollution in the Thames.

The Central Electricity Generating Board has shown enthusiastic co-operation, especially at the Kingsnorth power station where a joint Kent Wildfowlers' Association/WAGBI/Kent Ornithological Society reserve has been established, and at West Thurrock power station where access to the wader roost on the ash ponds and the cooling water intake screens was arranged, and in discussions over the siting of the proposed new power station at Barking. The opportunity of a helicopter survey of the Medway Estuary has also been provided.

The London Rowing Club kindly allowed us the use of their launch *Casamajor*, which enabled us to carry out detailed surveys of the reaches above London Bridge and further down river to Tilbury whenever the weather was favourable. To A. Johnson and W. Barling we must also express our sincere thanks for boatwork on the Medway, without which it would not have been possible to complete the surveys there. Our pilot on photographic flights over the North Kent Marshes and Essex has been D. B. Jones and we are extremely grateful to him for his skilful flying.

14

ACKNOWLEDGEMENTS

John Swift, Assistant Director, Conservation and Research, WAGBI provided the details of his analyses of wildfowl and wader foods on the Inner Thames. He was also the organiser for our trips with *Casamajor* as a member of the London Rowing Club. J. H. Price and I. Tittley, British Museum (Natural History) kindly provided us with a summary of their study of the algal population of the Inner Thames. Most of the data on the returning fish population of the Inner Thames are drawn from the detailed study by Dr A. Wheeler of the British Museum (Natural History), without which our knowledge of this most important part of the Inner Thames story would be minimal. To all we extend our most sincere thanks.

All the photographs have been taken by Dr Pamela Harrison, with the exception of plate 23 of Pintail and Mallard feeding on *Tubifex* which was taken by G. C. D. Harrison, for which we are most grateful.

A great many people have helped by providing details of their observations and information in the various areas described. Without them the picture would have been far less detailed. Our very sincere thanks are due to them all.

The Inner Thames: R. E. Alderton, R. Blindell, J. H. Brock, John F. Burton, K. A. Collett, M. Garside, R. W. George, F. J. Holroyde, R. C. Homes, D. Martin, B. S. Meadows, K. Noble, P. J. Oliver, K. C. Osborne, Capt. and Frau U. Schneider, De Heer and Mevrouw J. van Vlissingen, De Heer and Mevrouw P. van Vlissingen, R. V. White and J. F. Willis. The Annual Bird Reports of the London Natural History Society and its book *Birds of the London Area* have been of immense value in providing a picture of birdlife of the Inner Thames past and present, and we are equally grateful to all the observers who have contributed their observations to these publications.

The North Kent Marshes – The Medway: A. Allison, J. Black, T. Bowley, W. F. A. and D. Buck, Major J. P. T. Burchell, P. Comben, Mr and Mrs K. Earnshaw, R. J. Elvy, G. Graves, Major R. D. Hale, J. Hales, the late Dr J. M. Harrison, R. Hawkins, J. Hoad, J. Horley, Capt. J. N. Humphreys, D. B. and R. Jones, R. Lamb, H. and W. Mouland, A. J. Nichols, R. Sumner, J. Sutton, C. Swan, J. P. M. Wardell, M. Webb and Capt. J. V. Wilkinson.

The Thames: L. Batchelor, Mrs P. Brown, Mr and Mrs J. Carter, J. Dockery, M. French, the late R. French, E. Gillham, G. C. D.

15

ACKNOWLEDGEMENTS

and Miss J. T. R. Harrison, M. Jenkins, Dr and Mrs S. Kauffmann, Miss J. and Miss S. Kauffmann, T. Long, J. Mackay, D. I. and R. Maclean, T. Proctor, R. E. Scott and E. Valder.

The Swale: B. Hawkes, D. Mackay and R. V. White. Also we must thank all contributors to the Kent Bird Reports of the Kent Ornithological Society, whose records for the North Kent Marshes have proved invaluable.

South Essex Coast: G. Hooper, R. Smith and G. Wilsher.

We gratefully acknowledge the encouragement and advice of Piers Burnett and Mrs S. Sampson of André Deutsch Ltd during the production of this book, which has been of great value to us.

Last, but by no means least, P.J.G. would like to add his special thanks to his wife, Denise Grant, for much help and encouragement during the preparation of this book, which has made the task very much easier. We would also like to thank Miss Vanda Salmon for her splendid efforts in typing the sections on the North Kent Marshes and the South Essex Coast.

INTRODUCTION

❧

SOME books are exciting to write; some their authors feel compelled to write. We are more than lucky, for *The Thames Transformed* comes into both of these categories, and furthermore we have had the thrill of going out onto the river and the saltmarshes to establish many of the facts and take the photographs which have enabled us to tell this story.

Part of the story – the devastation of the Inner Thames by pollution, its ultimate restoration and the subsequent return of fish and waterfowl – has never been told fully before, simply because such an astonishing thing has never been achieved before. This is something in which Britain leads the world, as was most evident when we gave an illustrated lecture on the subject to the Fifth International Conference on the Conservation of Wetlands and Waterfowl, held in West Germany in 1974. This resulted in a congratulatory recommendation being sent from the thirty-five nations attending the Conference addressed to the two organisations primarily responsible for this triumph – the Port of London Authority and the Greater London Council. It was an appropriate moment for such a gesture, for it coincided very closely with the formation of the Thames Water Authority, to which the PLA and the GLC have now handed over their responsibilities for the well-being of the river.

But this is a story in two parts, for no account of the waterfowl on the Thames can be complete without describing the Outer Thames from Tilbury to Foulness on the northern shore and to Shellness at the eastern end of the Isle of Sheppey on the southern shore. Included in this great complex of the Thames Estuary, therefore, are the Swale channel and the Medway Estuary which, together with the Kentish shore of the Thames, form the famous North Kent Marshes, which are of immense international importance for their waterfowl. The Medway Estuary like the Inner Thames has also been transformed in recent years and is now by far the most important small estuary in Britain for its waterfowl.

17

Another area which might have been transformed – devastated would be a better word – was, of course, Foulness, which seemed in the early 1970's to be a virtual certainty for the site of London's third airport with an adjoining seaport. The loss of Foulness would have been a major disaster for waterfowl; it is the most important wintering ground for the Russian brent goose in western Europe, quite apart from its massive wading bird population.

The case put forward by the opponents of the scheme, including, of course, conservationists, was brilliantly conducted against what looked like insuperable odds, but the need for a third London airport, if it ever existed, has now faded completely behind the clouds of inflation.

The Thames Estuary may be likened to a trumpet pointing directly across the North Sea towards the Low Countries, the distant waterfowl breeding grounds in the Baltic and the mighty Russian tundras beyond. Little wonder, then, that at the time of autumn migration, when hosts of waterfowl are forced to move south-westwards along the great western European flyway, to avoid the winter's freeze, they funnel into the Thames trumpet waiting to receive them.

It is our responsibility to the international community to see that we have adequate wintering grounds to greet these waterfowl and to ensure that the great majority can return home in the spring to reproduce their kind.

That is why the International Waterfowl Research Bureau has been formed and is flourishing; this is where East meets West in full accord, for like the waterfowl, those of us who care for their future recognise no international limitations to our efforts and we have all come to work together in harmony and good will.

There is yet another reason why we have felt compelled to write this book, for the potential threats to the unspoilt outer estuary of London's river are, it seems, unending. That was why in 1971, when the whole vitally important southern shore of the Medway Estuary was threatened with destruction for a Maritime Industrial Development Area, the Fourth International Conference on the Conservation of Wetlands and Waterfowl, meeting in Iran, passed a recommendation addressed to the United Kingdom Government urging that the Medway Estuary should be excluded from such projects.

This was the first time that the authorities responsible for the future of the North Kent Marshes realised the international involvement, for twenty-three countries were represented at that

Conference, from Europe, Asia and Africa, together with representatives from the specialised agencies of the United Nations, namely UNESCO and FAO, together with independent organisations such as IUCN, ICBP, IWRB and the World Wildlife Fund.

Some might argue that, if the waterfowl can return to the Inner Thames so dramatically, then it is unnecessary to save the remaining unspoilt marshes beside the estuaries. We would like to be quite definite about this, for we do hold the strongest views on it. First, it must be recognised that the numbers and diversity of species using the Inner Thames cannot be compared (except for pochard) with the far greater numbers on the outer estuaries, while such magnificent birds as white-fronted and brent geese, wigeon and shoveler, which abound on the outer estuaries, are seldom found on the Inner Thames and nothing can be done to alter this. Industrial development has destroyed for ever the wilderness of marshland which they must have.

This brings us to the second point we would like to make in this respect. Although the sight of flocks of pochard, pintail and shelduck seen against a backcloth of London's dockland, Barking's power station or the tower blocks of Thamesmead will never cease to astonish and delight us (and indeed they bring London's waterfront alive for those who have to live and work beside it) they can never be quite as inspiring as in their proper habitat, which is the open marsh beyond. The area we are considering in this book covers approximately 110 miles of river front or coastline, of which more than half has been built over. The remaining unspoiled marshland is unique; it is a source of immense pleasure to a very large number of people – birdwatchers, wildfowlers, fishermen, sailors and those who just like to escape from towns and cities and enjoy the solitude and vista of flat open marshland and wonderful skies.

Surely it is not too much to ask for the remaining unspoilt marshes and fleets, mudbanks and creeks to be left for all to enjoy? Wetlands are not wastelands – though there are some who see them only as empty spaces on the map, to be reclaimed by refuse disposal and developed as quickly as possible. They are, in reality, priceless natural assets in a fast degrading world.

Those who would seek further to destroy such places as these marshes must realise the full value of what they are about to destroy, for their vital importance, both nationally and internationally, can no longer be denied. Now is the time to cry 'Enough!' in this overcrowded south-east England of ours, or we must answer to future generations, both at home and overseas, for what we have done.

19

INTRODUCTION

Appropriately, the publication of *The Thames Transformed* coincides with the European Wetlands Campaign 1976, a year in which the Council of Europe is devoting its efforts in nature conservation towards the correct management and true value of wetland habitats.

Let us remember that conservation is for man and that conservationists are not cranks. A goose does not appreciate that it is being conserved. It is being conserved by us for our enjoyment. We are not opposed to development, but only to development in the wrong places. Ours are voices crying for the wilderness and its wildlife, a swelling chorus coming from more and more, so that man can be refreshed through that peace of mind which comes from the solitude of such places.

Jeffery Harrison

Peter Grant

Pamela Harrison.

PART I
THE INNER THAMES

CHAPTER 1

THE GREAT CLEAN-UP

❧

ON such famous wildfowl havens as the Dutch polders or the marshes of southern France the spectacle which met our eyes would not have been so surprising. A fast moving motor boat had cut through a vast raft of pochard and sent them skywards in a flurry of wings and water. There were at least 4,000 in the gathering, now joined by smaller numbers of tufted duck, pintail and shelduck. A splendid sight anywhere, but this was the River Thames near the Woolwich Ferry, just a few miles downriver from the very heart of London, where the presence of these birds was tangible evidence of a miraculous transformation. As peace returned, groups broke off from the mass and returned again to the water against an incongruous backdrop of industrial riverside. It seemed that they brought with them a breath of fresh air to enliven and colour the panorama of cranes, factories and power stations. And this was no isolated event. Each winter now, the urbanised tideway between London and Tilbury is host to a large population of wildfowl and wading birds of a wide variety of species. Their presence is a climax to a remarkable story.

As recently as the early 1960's, an account of the birdlife of the Inner Thames would have made depressing reading. A few paragraphs would have been enough to describe how decades of pollution had reduced the teeming wildlife of past centuries to a pitiful state of near extinction. Fortunately an efficient anti-pollution programme has been in operation since 1959 and its effect on the general health of the river and its fish and bird populations has been spectacular. Instead of a gloomy picture of a river rendered lifeless by gross pollution, we are able to describe a unique and heartening achievement. For the first time in the world, a heavily polluted and industrialised river has been restored to such a degree that waterfowl and fish have returned in abundance. That such a transformation has taken place so rapidly, in a situation which at first seemed quite

23

hopeless, gives encouragement to even the most pessimistic wildlife conservationist.

A blueprint for the restoration of polluted waterways has been established, hopefully to be followed in other parts of the world where such problems exist. The story is a tribute to the foresight and dedication of those involved in the scheme, particularly the Port of London Authority and the Greater London Council, and the riverside industries which have readily cooperated in its implementation.

THE PHYSICAL SETTING

It is the Inner Thames, the twenty-five miles between London Bridge and Tilbury, which has benefitted most from the anti-pollution campaign. The narrows of this section received the pollution which poured out of London, without any of the dilution from the sea which lessened its impact in the outer estuary. The Thames widens gradually from about 100 yards in the centre of London to about 800 yards in the lower reaches. Extensive areas of mud are uncovered at low tide on the inner banks of the river bends and in the larger bays. Towards the centre of London the intertidal zone becomes progressively narrower and more shingly. Between London and Woolwich, about half the total length of this section, the riverside is completely built up: factories, power stations, oil installations, wharves and innumerable jetties and piers form a completely artifical waterfront. In recent years large riverside housing developments have replaced obsolete commercial and industrial buildings.

Below Woolwich the river broadens, and although the open estuary is a further twenty-five miles downriver, the Inner Thames takes on a more estuarine character. As the river approaches Tilbury the effects of salinity are first noted and the flora and fauna of the river increasingly show a marine influence. There are welcome breaks in the urbanisation, and remnants of the once extensive Thames-side marshes, now drained and largely used as grazing pasture, provide a welcome rural atmosphere in places, although such areas continue to be eroded by industrial and housing developments and rubbish tips.

On the river itself there have been major changes in recent years. Containerisation and the introduction of much larger ships has led to a gradual run-down of the docks near the centre of London. The docks at Tilbury, deepened, enlarged and modernised, now handle

24

the vast majority of trade, and the Inner Thames has lost much of the bustle of commercial shipping which typified it until the 1960's. Hand-in-hand with this trend has come the closure and demolition of riverside industrial and commercial buildings associated with the shipping which now goes elsewhere. To those who knew the river in its heyday as a great artery of commerce it is now often strangely quiet in the reaches near London, and much of the waterfront has an air of dereliction. But all is rapid change as new buildings, mainly housing, mushroom in place of the old.

Although the character of the Inner Thames may be changing, it is still very much an urban, industrialised river, and it is in this apparently inhospitable setting that the miraculous wildlife transformation has taken place. To appreciate the extent of the success we must first go back and look at the history of the Thames and its virtual destruction as an ecological entity.

DEVELOPMENT AND POLLUTION – THE DECLINE OF WILDLIFE

There is no doubt that before the spread of London and the Industrial Revolution the Inner Thames must have been a magnificent area for wildlife. Much of the shore was a wilderness of marshes and reed beds, harbouring such present-day rarities as bitterns and bearded reedlings. Spoonbills nested in the area of Putney Bridge up to the sixteenth century, and Montagu's and marsh harriers quartered the marshes of South London around Bermondsey up to the early 1800's. The waters supported a thriving fishing industry based on Billingsgate and attracted a run of salmon and sea trout. Much of the decline took place in the early nineteenth century; partly because of increasing pollution, but mainly as a result of the reclamation of huge areas of riverside marsh. This low-lying ground was ideal for the construction of large dock systems. Between 1800 and 1810 the Surrey Docks were enlarged and the first of the London and India Docks was opened. Subsequent dock openings were St Katherine's in 1828, West India in 1829, Victoria in 1855, Millwall in 1868, Royal Albert in 1880 and Tilbury in 1886. This timetable marks both the increasing commercial importance of the Thames and the destruction of its riverside habitats and their wildlife.

While the construction of the docks, together with the spread of riverside housing and industry, greatly reduced the wildlife of the river marshes, it was growing pollution which brought about the eventual decline of the fish and birdlife of the tideway itself. Although the river had been used since Roman times as a convenient place to dispose of London's waste, the problem did not reach excessive proportions until the 1800's. Then the growing population combined with the increasing use of the newly-invented water closet, quickly led to overloading of the existing sewage disposal system. In those days sewage 'disposal' was something of a euphemism: effluent, often untreated, was channelled directly into the Thames and its tributaries through a miscellany of sewer outlets and outdated sewage works. It was not disposal at all. Instead the effluent was trapped in the narrows of the river, by the ebb and flow of the tides, taking weeks or even months before it finally escaped to the open estuary. The construction of a massive new sewer system in the early 1860's, criss-crossing London and leading to the great outfalls at Beckton and Crossness, alleviated the situation only temporarily. Treatment of the effluent was still inadequate, and the location of the new outfalls within the river narrows meant that little more had been done than to shift the problem a few miles further downstream.

The state of the river deteriorated steadily over the years with what was, perhaps, the final blow coming during the Second World War when major sewage works and sewers were damaged or destroyed. During the 1940's and 1950's the health of the Thames was at its lowest ebb. The river was little better than an open sewer; the water was black in colour, contained no oxygen, and during the summer months the foul smell from the Thames was detectable over a wide area. While this made things unpleasant for people living near the river, for wildlife it meant that the death knell had been sounded. Only the most specialised forms of water life could survive in the anaerobic conditions. The surface was littered with rafts of rubbish and driftwood (a major hazard to small craft) and great banks of detergent foam. The once teeming fish had finally been driven out, apart from a few eels which were able to survive because of their ability to breathe air direct from the surface. The birdlife of the inner, built-up reaches between London and Woolwich was reduced to a handful of mallard and mute swans, and they owed their existence to spillages from the grain wharves rather than a natural food supply. Gulls of a variety of species, however, seemed to thrive and probably owed much of the success of their colonisation of London (which had gained pace since the end of the nineteenth century) to their scavenging feeding habits in the sewer-like conditions.

The lack of birds during the height of the pollution meant that the river did not attract the attention of many birdwatchers. The reservoirs and sewage farms of London and the marshes further out in the estuary were a much greater draw. Fortunately the remnants of the once extensive Thames-side marshes at Greenwich, Woolwich, Dartford and Swanscombe were quite closely watched. These areas, unaffected by the pollution in the river itself, contained habitats attractive to birds and supported a surprisingly interesting variety of species for places so close to London. Incidental observations of the Thames and its foreshore made during visits to these areas provide a good overall picture of the birdlife during this period, and draw a valuable baseline with which to compare the present situation. The most comprehensive summary is provided by John F. Burton who, with others, regularly studied the Inner Thames marshes between 1945 and 1950. In his six years of study he found that wildfowl rarely penetrated further upstream than Erith. Of the eight species of duck which he saw on the river, none normally exceeded a flock size of ten. Even in conditions of severe cold, when many thousands are displaced from their continental feeding grounds by ice, the largest flock ever seen was fifty-five teal during the 1949/50 winter. Of fifteen species of waders, only six were considered as regular visitors to the mud foreshore of the river, and of these only lapwing and snipe ventured above Erith. Redshank were generally the most numerous with flocks totalling around a hundred between Dartford and Swanscombe, while numbers of dunlin, curlew, snipe and ringed plovers rarely exceeded twenty.

The observations of another ornithologist, Jeremy H. Brock, show that the birdless state of the Inner Thames continued right up to the period between 1960 and 1966. It was during these years that the clean-up programme began to have effect and birds began to edge their way in larger numbers into the lower reaches around Swanscombe and Dartford as the quality of the water began to improve. This improvement had yet to extend as far as Rainham, where the only duck which Brock saw on the river itself were mallard, and then never in numbers greater than thirty. The laboratory where he worked at Beckton overlooked the Thames and enabled a close watch to be kept on the Barking Reach and, on the opposite side of the river, the Woolwich bay. Yet during the whole seven years these sites were completely devoid of any flocks of duck or waders.

That was the sorry plight of birds on the Inner Thames during the black years of pollution. Who would have believed then the dramatic reversal which was about to take place? Within ten years those same reaches of the river were to be transformed from a virtual avian void to a refuge for many species of water birds, including a wintering population of up to 10,000 wildfowl and 12,000 waders.

THE FIGHT AGAINST POLLUTION

The clean-up programme which brought about the miracle was, to say the least, long overdue. Since the early nineteenth century the need to combat the pollution of the river had become increasingly obvious, yet the measures taken were piecemeal and ineffective, or at best improved the situation only temporarily. It was the commercial interests of the rapidly expanding city which invariably took precedence over the voice of the minority concerned with the unhealthy environment which was being created. It seemed that London was prepared to accept the state of affairs which existed until conditions became so chronic that they put an end to complacency. So the history of pollution control on the Thames was, until recently, one of cure rather than prevention based on forward planning.

The first crisis point was reached during the 1850's, and conditions became particularly bad during the long hot summer of 1856 which became notorious as 'The Year of the Great Stink'. This state resulted from sewage discharges into the Thames from the newly constructed sewer systems. Instead of being disposed of on the fields around London, as had mainly been the practice before, the effluent was deposited over the foreshore and into the river. The central reaches through London rapidly degenerated into an open sewer. The situation literally forced itself on the government of the day: disinfectant soaked sheets had to be hung at the windows of the Houses of Parliament to counteract the stench. Water intakes, which previously had supplied one third of London's needs, had to be sealed off or moved well above the polluted zone. The thriving Thames fishery was wiped out. Such conditions, and major outbreaks of water-borne disease such as cholera (14,000 people died in the epidemic of 1848/49), emphasised the need for action.

In 1857 a new organisation, the Thames Conservancy, came into being vested with powers to prohibit pollution of the river. Its jurisdiction, however, did not extend to the control of sewage disposal. It was thought that this facet of the problem was being effectively dealt with by the construction of new intercepting sewers north and south of the river to carry the effluent away from central

London to large outfalls at Beckton and Crossness. This work, carried out by the Metropolitan Board of Works under the direction of Sir Joseph Bazalgette, was largely completed in 1864. The project, which had cost in excess of £4 million and had at times employed over 6,000 men, was formally opened with much ceremony in April 1865 by HRH the Prince of Wales, later Edward VII, before numerous State and Church dignitaries. The sewers, pumping stations and engineering works were constructed in classically ornate Victorian style, and much of the system is still in use, a tribute to the skill of the engineers of the day. Abbey Mills pumping station – still working to this day – is a magnificent example of their work.

In central London the success of the scheme was complete. The state of the river was improved to such an extent that the foul conditions of the 1850's have never returned to this day, and some fish were able to make a welcome, though short-lived, comeback. Downriver in the vicinity of the new outfalls, however, all was far from well. At Barking there were numerous complaints about the unsatisfactory state of the river soon after the new outfalls had come into operation. An enquiry into the great loss of life sustained in the sinking of the pleasure boat *Princess Alice* in 1878 concluded that the deaths had been accelerated by the putrid state of the water off the Beckton outfall where the accident occurred. With the continuing spread of London it was not long before the major outfalls were within the boundaries of the metropolis, and soon they became greatly overloaded by a doubling of London's population to nearly five million between 1840 and 1880. As a result of a Royal Commission set up in 1882, new treatment methods were employed at Beckton and Crossness, involving the settling out of solid matter from the sewage effluent and its disposal at sea. But these actions did little more than put off to a later date the real solution of the problem.

The responsibility for the conservancy of the Thames was eventually transferred to the Port of London Authority on its formation in 1909. Further efforts were made to bring back life to what was rapidly becoming a totally dead river, including the introduction of new plant at Beckton which not only settled out the solid matter, but also treated the remaining fluids to obtain a cleaner discharge into the Thames. Despite such action the overall condition of the waters of the tidal Thames continued its downward trend. In the late 1940's, the situation was once again brought to crisis point by widespread damage to sewers and sewage works sustained during the Second World War. For a long time money was not available to carry out repairs, let alone essential improvements. The Port of London Authority and the London County Council jointly pressed for new powers and direction to combat the problem. As a result a special committee was formed in 1949 to survey the Thames under the Water Pollution Research Board, and in 1951 a Governmental Committee was appointed under the chairmanship of Professor A. J. Sutton Pippard to examine the effects of pollutant discharges into the Thames. Such was the complexity of the problems that the findings of these committees were not published until the early 1960's.

As a result of these investigations the special problems of the Thames, in relation to its large pollutant load in an enclosed tidal system, were much more fully understood, and for the first time a phased programme of effective improvement could be envisaged and acted upon. The effect of pollutants on the amount of dissolved oxygen in the river was shown to be of major importance. In cases of acute pollution, the oxygen content can be entirely removed by the decomposition of organic pollutants such as sewage effluent. When this anaerobic state is reached the aggressive and foul-smelling hydrogen sulphide is produced, the same 'rotting eggs' ingredient of practical jokers' stink bombs. It was this gas which gave the Thames its characteristic stench during the worst periods of pollution.

Another important consideration was the 'retention period' of the river, that is to say the length of time taken for a body of water to reach the open sea from a given point within the river narrows. Largely because of the ebb and flow of its twice-daily tides, the Thames has a surprisingly long retention period. An item dropped into the river at London Bridge, for example, will take twenty days to float forty miles to the sea even during periods of heavy fresh water flow. In periods of low rainfall when the flow of fresh water is low it can take up to eighty days. This greatly worsened the effect of the sewage effluent, which remained trapped in the river narrows for long periods instead of being 'flushed through' quickly to the open sea.

The better understanding of these particular problems led the investigators to make an early recommendation for the improvement of the main sewage works at Beckton and Crossness. These suggestions were acted upon by the London County Council and its successor, the Greater London Council, and in 1964 a greatly enlarged new works was opened at Crossness, and similar work at Beckton was completed in 1974.

The most up-to-date filtration, treatment and aeration equipment was installed at these new works, so that nowadays the final fluid discharge to the Thames is virtually pure water. The solid matter is now treated in such a way as to render it almost sterile and non-toxic, and it continues to be dumped far out in the estuary by special ships. London's sewage disposal system has been further improved by the GLC's programme of closing many small and inefficient local sewage works. The flow from these has been redirected through the larger, modernised regional works; and since these discharge into the Thames, either directly or via its tributaries, the river has benefitted greatly. In 1935 there were 190 sewage works within a twenty-five mile radius of the centre of London; by 1970 these had been reduced to twelve main regional works.

The Water Pollution Research Board had identified the major sources of pollution in the Thames as follows:

Sewage works (domestic and industrial waste) .	79%
Industrial discharges (direct to the river) . .	12%
Upper Thames	4%
Tributaries	3%
Storm Water	2%

The need for an improved sewage disposal system can be clearly seen, and the fact that by 1970 Beckton and Crossness were alone responsible for the treatment of over sixty per cent of London's sewage flow underlines the importance of the modernisation there. These improvements cost the Greater London Council and several smaller local authorities an estimated £45 million.

While London's sewage disposal system is now adequate for the vast majority of the time, and further improvements are planned, it does not have a safety margin enough to handle massive flows of surface water which occur from time to time as a result of freak rain storms. In such conditions the present sewers are unable to cope, and the excess, together with the untreated sewage which it carries with it, is discharged direct to the river through storm sewers, resulting in rapid oxygen loss in the river.

The last such incident occurred on 20th June, 1973, when the dissolved oxygen was depleted to a maximum of ten per cent for the whole river from Barnes to Crossness, resulting in a large fish mortality in the reaches above London. Fish took a long time to recover, and few were found in the central reaches for many months after. Clearly this could prove a serious obstacle to the establishment of a permanent fish population in the river until such time as an

31

ample oxygen reserve is established to compensate in such freak rainfall.

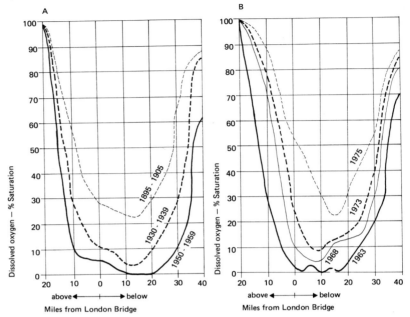

Figure 1. Third quarter oxygen sag curves for the Thames. On the left, the deteriorating situation, 1895–1905 to 1950–59. On the right, the improving situation shown by the curves for 1963, 1968, 1973 and 1975.

A further important result of the investigating committees' findings was the strengthening of the Port of London Authority's control over pollution. By 1968, the PLA had full pollution control of the tidal river between Teddington and the estuary, and this responsibility was backed up by powerful new laws. No one could discharge other than uncontaminated surface water without first applying for PLA consent, which was given only subject to stringent controls over quality and volume and regular checks on the discharge. In bad cases industrial effluents had to be channelled into the main sewer system where they could be better handled. Overall the reaction of riverside industry to these controls has been one of cooperation, and in some cases great expense and effort have been expended to comply with the new standards. In the case of the Thames Board Mills of Purfleet, for example, it was not possible for various reasons to bring their effluent up to the required level, nor divert its flow to the sewers. As an alternative, another solution to the problem was employed. The company bore the research and development costs of a unique aerator which oxygenates the river in sufficient quantities to over-compensate for the oxygen depletion caused by their effluent.

Paper manufacturing plants like that of Thames Board Mills have provided a particular pollution problem in the Thames, which has six such plants along its banks. Large volumes of water are used in the manufacturing process, and it is returned to the river largely de-oxygenated and carrying a suspension of wood pulp and other paper ingredients.

An aerator of the type installed by Thames Board Mills is an ideal answer in the short term, but in the long term it becomes progressively less effective. As the general oxygen levels increase, the potential oxygen transfer from aerator to river is correspondingly decreased, so that the original aim of compensating for the oxygen depletion of the effluent is lost.

Treatment of the effluent itself before discharge is the only

1. The Thames Board Mills' oxygenation plant at Erith which, at the moment, more than compensates for the deoxygenation caused by discharges from the factory.

permanent solution, and at the Bowater Scott factory at Northfleet a new land-based 'coagulation plant' has been installed, which removes the suspended solids from the effluent. The pulp salvaged by this process has been found suitable for manufacturing certain types of packaging cartons, an unexpected further advantage of this process.

It was not long before the effect of all this activity began to show itself in tangible form. Between 1953 and 1962 the polluting load of the river had been cut by seventeen per cent and by 1969 it had dropped by a further twenty-three per cent. The improving quality of the river can best be shown by data on the amount of dissolved oxygen contained in the water, records of which have been kept by the Greater London Council and its predecessors since 1893. Figure shows the declining situation up to 1959 and the subsequent gradual improvement from 1963. These 'oxygen sag curves' are based on samples taken in the third quarter of the year (when levels are at their lowest due to minimum rainfall thus less dilution from fresh water flow) and higher temperatures (which inhibit the rate of natural oxygen absorption at the surface), thus they show the situation at its worst in each year. Not only is the increase in oxygen demonstrated, but also, and just as important, the gradual narrowing of the 'plug' of heavily polluted water in the central sections of the Inner Thames.

The latest sag curve, that for the third quarter of 1975, shows a remarkable situation. Despite very low fresh water flows as a result of minimal rainfall during the summer the average minimum dissolved oxygen was twenty-one per cent compared with eleven per cent for the same period in 1974. This is a much greater degree of oxygenation than has ever been predicted in the foreseeable future for the Thames, indeed the target set at the instigation of the clean-up programme was a level of ten per cent dissolved oxygen at all times of the year by 1980! That this has been exceeded by such a large margin so far ahead of the target year is some measure of the effectiveness of the original plan and the later modifications.

If these levels can be maintained, and with the further planned sewage works improvements this should be possible, then the oxygen reserve is adequate to deal with temporary emergencies such as storm water surges. And the target of thirty per cent dissolved oxygen which should allow the passage of migrant salmon on a regular basis is well within sight. The 1975 oxygen levels show a better situation than has existed at any time previously during the present century.

Given that concentrations of toxic pollutants do not reach harmful proportions, a degree of oxygenation in the water is the one essential for fish and aquatic plant life to survive. Indirectly this benefits creatures higher up the food chain, fish-eating terns and cormorants, for example.

Warm water discharges from the cooling system of the twenty Thames-side power stations have an indirect pollutant effect. They are all 'directly cooled' stations, that is to say they use water drawn from the river which is subsequently returned at a greater temperature after passing through the cooling system. Without any power stations the average summer temperature of the river would be around 18° to 19°C, whereas the actual temperature is 22°C. The polluting effect of this increased temperature is twofold. Firstly the natural absorption of oxygen at the surface is slowed down, and secondly the decomposition of organic pollutants is accelerated so that the existing oxygen content is used up proportionately faster. The oxygen 'sag curve' for the third quarter of the year is three to four per cent lower at its lowest point than it would be if there were no power stations.

The present combined output capacity of the existing power stations is just over 6,500 megawatts. Four much larger new power stations are planned for Thames-side sites before the end of the present century, with a combined output capacity of nearly 7,000 megawatts. If they are directly cooled as with the existing stations the average summer temperature of the river will be increased to 26°C, and the dissolved oxygen depletion would be a further five to six per cent.

An alternative method of cooling power stations is with cooling towers, in which the same water is circulated over and over again, being cooled for re-use in each cycle in the massive cooling towers. In this method only a small intake of water is required to make up the loss from evaporation, and there is no discharge of heated water. It is more expensive than direct cooling, and the massive towers can be unsightly. The first of the new power stations, to come into full operation in 1981 at Littlebrook, has been designed as a directly cooled station, but clearly serious consideration should be given to permitting only tower cooled stations in the future.

Another type of pollution, that of detergents, is also an important consideration as far as wildlife is concerned. The increasing use of household detergents since the 1940's has posed its own special problems to those trying to improve the river. It is widely believed that the advent of detergents was a major blow to the worsening state of the Thames, and that they provided the last straw which brought about the completely anaerobic state of the river in the 1950's. The old methods of sewage treatment were unable to remove detergents, and as a result high concentrations escaped through sewage discharges to form unsightly masses of foam in the Thames and its tributaries. Boat crews have told us that the problem was especially marked in the dry summer of 1959 when craft moored near the Woolwich Ferry were completely submerged in mountains of foam stirred up by the continual movement of the ferry boats. The immediate effect of detergents is to greatly reduce the rate at which oxygen can be transferred by aeration systems into activated sludge. When the detergent had passed through into the waterways it left a film on the surface and continued to inhibit the natural absorption of oxygen at the surface. As well as being toxic to fish the film of detergent on the surface would deter wildfowl as it would break down the natural waterproofing of their plumage. The present day use of biodegradable 'soft' detergents which were introduced by the manufacturers to combat this major problem have greatly eased the danger, and this combined with new and more effective treatment methods, has now minimised the adverse effects of detergents.

So pollution has at last been brought under control, and the Inner Thames is once more a living river. It must be hoped that the future will see continued vigilance and improvements. Since April 1974 responsibility for pollution control has passed from the Port of London Authority to the new Thames Water Authority. Oil pollution remains the concern of the Port of London Authority. New, higher goals of purity have been set, which may enable migratory fish to pass through to the upper reaches, and a biological monitoring programme has been initiated. In 1975 a new pollution control vessel *Thameswater* was launched, which will not only sample the water of the tidal Thames, but is also fitted with a grab which will enable the river bed to be sampled at depths of up to a hundred feet. The TWA has taken up its responsibilities with an enthusiasm which bodes well for the future.

The beneficial effects of the anti-pollution programme are not confined to birds, although that is what we are mainly concerned with here. The Thames is now a river fit for humans to live by: no longer is the water black and stinking and a worrying health hazard. The land vacated by industry which has moved away from the area can now be used for large-scale housing developments, something impossible to contemplate in the past. Greater leisure use of the Thames can be envisaged now that it is clean again.

Wildlife other than birds has benefitted, and the return of fish to the Inner Thames is the most striking example and this has received a good deal of publicity. This aspect has been closely studied by Dr Alwynne Wheeler of the British Natural History Museum. In a thorough survey undertaken in 1957 he found that in normal conditions the whole forty miles of river between Richmond and Tilbury was devoid of fish, apart from eels which were able to survive in the anaerobic conditions because of their ability to take air at the surface.

Fish began to return in 1963, coinciding with the first arrivals of birds. In 1965 live fish were caught for the first time on the screens of the cooling water intake of Fulham power station, and this chance suggested an effective way of monitoring the increasing fish fauna of the river. By 1967 Dr Wheeler had organised a regular survey of fish caught at the intake screens of seven power stations along the river. This gave a valuable cross-section from the fresh water upstream conditions at Fulham power station to the near marine conditions at West Thurrock power station. The survey continued until the end of 1973, when it was taken over by the Thames Water Authority. By the end of 1975 no less than eighty-six species of fresh water and marine fish had been identified, a total made even more remarkable by the fact that in 1957 the same reaches of the Thames had been virtually fishless.

Some species are numerous even in the central reaches, where the Greater London Council now organises an annual fishing competition.

As well as the long list of species, two particular aspects of the return of fish are especially significant. Firstly, the river is being used increasingly as a 'nursery' by some species: tiny flounders have been found in the upper reaches having 'migrated' through the central reaches from the estuary where they were spawned, and elvers (which unlike adult eels are most sensitive to pollution) only 2½ to 3 inches long have been found as far upriver as Hammersmith, and in large numbers in some of the creeks and ditches along the Inner Thames. Secondly, now that the highly polluted 'plug' of water in the central reaches has been eliminated, it has enabled migratory species such as the smelt and brown or sea trout to pass through to the reaches above London, along with several marine species such as the flounder, sand goby, sprat and sand eel. This provides tangible proof that fish can now survive through the worst polluted zones downstream.

Two salmon have recently been taken in the lower reaches of the Inner Thames. The first of these was caught on the intake screen of the West Thurrock power station in November 1974, the first in the Thames for over 100 years. This has given hope that with continued improvements the Thames could well become a thriving salmon river as it has been in the past. Salmon are especially sensitive to pollution and it has been estimated that they will not tolerate a dissolved oxygen level of less than thirty per cent through which to 'migrate'. Records of salmon caught at Taplow Mill in Buckinghamshire show that between 1794 and 1821, a total of 483 were taken of a combined weight of over 7,000 lbs. The best years were 1801 and 1804 when over sixty fish were caught. Some idea of the total salmon catch from the Thames is given by records of 130 sold at Billingsgate market in a single day in 1766. The London naturalist William Yarrell reported the last Thames-caught salmon known to him as being taken in June, 1833, but there were very occasional further records known until about 1860.

Until the early 1800's the Thames supported a thriving fishing industry based on Billingsgate, London's fish market. As well as salmon the other major commercial fish were smelt, lamperns, and whitebait. The days may still be a long way off when commercial fishing can return, although Essex-based fishing boats have been able to take increasingly large catches well inside the estuary in recent years. The fact that the Inner Thames now contains a thriving fish population at all times of the year must be regarded as a major and heartening step in the right direction.

With present trends of improving oxygen levels in the Thames, the return of salmon in good numbers is a real and exciting prospect. The dissolved oxygen levels of 1975, with the average third-quarter minimum of twenty-one per cent, suggests that the requisite level of thirty per cent may not be as far off as was originally estimated. Besides an adequate oxygen level in the water this would also be dependent on the introduction of large numbers of newly hatched salmon to the headwaters of the Thames, so that eventually the adult fish would home on their 'natal' area to spawn. At present there are barriers to their progress on their return journey up the Thames in the form of locks. These would presumably have to be by-passed by fish-ladders. Perhaps a more practical initial step would be to introduce the newly hatched salmon to the Darent, a tributary of the Thames which joins at Dartford Creek. This tributary has no barriers for the returning adults, and proposed improvements to the Long Reach sewage works will greatly improve the quality of the water in the area. Gravel pits near the head of the Darent at Sevenoaks would be an ideal introduction point for the young fish, and eventually the gravelly bottoms of the pits would provide an ideal spawning ground.

The improved state of the Thames is also reflected by the increased growth and upriver spread of various species of marine algae or seaweeds over the past ten years. In the years of worst pollution the embankments and pilings of the Inner Thames were almost devoid of any prolific algal growths, but recent studies have shown a marked improvement in the situation, akin to the recolonisation of the river by birds and fish. The most readily visible evidence of this trend may be seen in the healthy and vigorous growths of the large brown fucoid algae, or bladder wracks, which may now be seen as far upriver as Crossness. The two species involved are *Fucus vesiculosus* and *F. spiralis*. Another genus of seaweeds, the green algae *Enteromorpha*, form much of the lush green growths which are now an obvious feature of the river walls and pilings along the whole length of the Inner Thames. Boat crews and other people who have been associated with the river for a long period frequently comment on the increased abundance and spread of the 'green seaweeds' in recent years, and we have noticed this ourselves in the comparatively short period of our study. Various species of *Enteromorpha* are involved, but the two most abundant are *E. prolifera* and *E. intestinalis*. The growths of *Enteromorpha* are an important food for mute swans, mallard, coot and moorhens on the Inner Thames, and other species of wildfowl probably feed on it to some extent.

Against all the beneficial effects of the cleaner Thames must be set a few adverse ones. The activities of a new and thriving population of wood-boring ship-worms *Toredo sp.* in the river have caused some damage to timber constructions set in the river, whereas this was never a problem during the polluted years. The large intake of fish and brown shrimps into the cooling water systems of riverside power stations, especially West Thurrock, sometimes causes a disposal problem. At times they have to be carted away by the barrow load to prevent the filter system from becoming overloaded. A remarkable turn of events from the situation which existed in the early 1960's when the capture of just one fish on the filter screens at West Thurrock was noteworthy!

CHAPTER 2

THE BIRDS RETURN

❧

LARGE flocks of wildfowl were seen for the first time on the Inner Thames during the cold winters at the beginning of the 1960's. There were teal flocks of up to 250 at Barking and 500 at Swanscombe, pochard up to 175 at Rainham and 500 at Swanscombe and shelduck up to 85 at Dartford and 500 at Swanscombe. All were completely without precedent on the Inner Thames. At the time the presence of these flocks was attributed to the spells of arctic weather, but in retrospect it seems that the cleaner river was also a contributory factor. The following winters were relatively mild, but they saw some further increases and upriver movement of the flocks. It was not until 1968/69, however, that some really dramatic developments took place.

We first became involved with the birds on the Inner Thames after Richard White had written to PJG describing a visit which he had made to the long bay at Woolwich on Christmas Day, 1968. He knew the birds of the Inner Thames and its marshes better than anyone, and clearly something quite extraordinary was happening: he reported two large flocks of pochard totalling 1,500, quite contented, with groups occasionally diving for food. With the pochard were small numbers of shelduck, pintail and tufted duck, all relatively unknown so far upriver, as well as some mallard. More surprising was the fact that they had arrived during mild weather, and that they were apparently resident in the area.

The presence of these birds posed some exciting questions. Why had they come to the Inner Thames when the area has been largely shunned by wildfowl in the past? What food was attracting them? What was the extent of the 'invasion'? Further downriver around Swanscombe, large flocks of waders, as well as wildfowl, had begun to appear, and this fact posed similar questions. Clearly some dramatic changes were occurring, and as our investigations progressed a remarkable and unique story unfolded. Some urgent

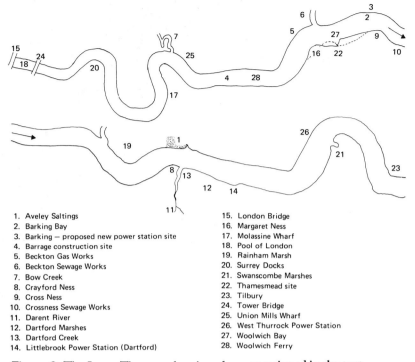

1. Aveley Saltings
2. Barking Bay
3. Barking — proposed new power station site
4. Barrage construction site
5. Beckton Gas Works
6. Beckton Sewage Works
7. Bow Creek
8. Crayford Ness
9. Cross Ness
10. Crossness Sewage Works
11. Darent River
12. Dartford Marshes
13. Dartford Creek
14. Littlebrook Power Station (Dartford)
15. London Bridge
16. Margaret Ness
17. Molassine Wharf
18. Pool of London
19. Rainham Marsh
20. Surrey Docks
21. Swanscombe Marshes
22. Thamesmead site
23. Tilbury
24. Tower Bridge
25. Union Mills Wharf
26. West Thurrock Power Station
27. Woolwich Bay
28. Woolwich Ferry

Figure 2. The Inner Thames, showing places mentioned in the text.

conservation needs of these birds also became apparent, and this aspect was later to form an additional important part of our studies.

By 1969/70, regular counts had been organised along the whole of the Inner Thames. These were made by many observers, working in teams and individually, and their results were correlated by the London Natural History Society and later as part of the national 'Birds of Estuaries' Enquiry, organised by the British Trust for Ornithology and the Royal Society for the Protection of Birds. Our own counts, made from the shore and also from regular boat trips on the river, augmented these data. Thus a thorough quantitative and qualitative monitoring programme was established from which we have been able to judge the subsequent population increases and upriver spread, and also the relative importance to wildfowl and waders of the various sites along the river.

It was clearly of major importance to establish at an early stage what was the main food attracting the wildfowl and waders, and a

2. Pochard over Barking Power Station. Pochard were the first species to move into the Inner Thames in large numbers.

programme of research was initiated in cooperation with the Wildfowlers' Association of Great Britain and Ireland, organised by the Association's Conservation/Research Officer, John Swift, and under licence from the Nature Conservancy. A full report on his findings is published in Appendix I. The discoveries emerging from this research were surprising. It appears that the main food of the wildfowl was various species of *Tubifex* worms, and that for many it was the first time that they had been known to take this food, moreover pochard were seen to change from their normal dive-feeding habits to dabbling, so that they could take full advantage of this food source. The abundance of *Tubifex* in some parts of the Thames foreshore can be demonstrated by a simple experiment: mud taken in handfuls at random and placed in an aquarium erupts into life once it has settled in a layer on the bottom. The thread-like red worms emerge in profusion from the mud, and the effect is like a field of waving red grass. Its attraction to the wildfowl was obvious, for they had only to dip their heads below the surface and 'graze' the *Tubifex*, or sift it from the mud by dabbling.

But that was only part of the answer, for we learned, to our dismay at first, that *Tubifex* thrive in the worst polluted rivers, and that it had been abundant in the Thames for years before the arrival of the wildfowl. Clearly there had been other changes which had enabled them to get at the already existing food supply. One important change in the state of the mud itself is that, due to the anti-pollution activity, it no longer contains the obnoxious hydrogen sulphide which gave the Thames foreshore its distinctive black colour and stench in the past. Although *Tubifex* could survive in such conditions, wildfowl could not get at the worms without stirring up the mud and releasing hydrogen sulphide which would certainly prove most distasteful. A further factor is likely to be the extent of detergent pollution: in the worst years of pollution a film of detergent covered the water of the Inner Thames, and this would certainly have had an adverse effect on the waterproofing of any wildfowl which settled for any length of time on the river. Other

3. Shelduck, pintail and mallard enliven the dockland scene.

factors may have been operating as well, but the main ones are clearly connected with lessening pollution; as is further demonstrated by the gradual upriver movements of some species corresponding from year to year with the gradually improving quality of the water.

4 Teal over Barking Bay at low tide.

For some species on the Inner Thames, especially mallard, mute swans, coot and moorhens, the green algae *Enteromorpha* provides additional food, or in the case of the last two, the main part of their diet. Improved oxygenation of the water has resulted in a great increase of this plant throughout the Inner Thames, and it now grows in profusion in the upper reaches towards London where it

44

could not exist before. All four species have been seen feeding on *Enteromorpha* on many occasions, especially on a rising tide when the water lifts it off the river walls and pilings, making it easy for the birds to 'graze'.

Other important wildfowl foods on the Inner Thames are grain spilled as barges are unloaded at grain wharves along the river, providing the main food of mute swans and some scavenging mallard, and grass, which is the major preference of wigeon on the Aveley saltings.

Of the waders, it appears that only dunlin can survive on a mainly *Tubifex* diet. This is suggested by the fact that it is the only wader species to have colonised the upper reaches of the Inner Thames above Rainham in large numbers, where *Tubifex* is the only abundant invertebrate to be found in the mud. Below Rainham there is a wider choice of invertebrate food, including *Nereid* worms which appear to form an important part of the diet of ringed plover, curlew, redshank and ruff.

The importance of *Tubifex* to the birds of the Inner Thames is readily apparent. It is likely that the continued success of the anti-pollution programme will lead to major changes in the *Tubifex* population which will in turn affect the birds in the future; indeed there are already strong signs that this is happening. So it is important to look at the factors which affect the distribution and abundance of tubificid worms in general.

Four species of tubificid worms are found commonly in the Thames. Two of these, *Tubifex tubifex* and *T. costatus* thrive in highly polluted water where the level of dissolved oxygen is less than ten per cent. *Limnodrilus hoffmeisteri* generally requires a level higher than ten per cent, and *Peloscolex benedeni* needs much higher levels at around twenty-five to thirty per cent.

The amount of salt in the water is also important: *T. tubifex* is a fresh water species which will tolerate only minimal salinity, while *L. hoffmeisteri* can tolerate slightly higher concentrations of salt. *T. costatus* can live in a wide range of salinities from almost fresh water to fully marine. *P. benedeni* lives in conditions varying from brackish to marine.

Other factors such as water temperature, sediment particle size, organic matter in the sediment, and predation also affect tubificid distribution, but oxygen and salt levels are of greatest importance in the Thames.

That there has been a major drop in the *Tubifex* population since 1975 is now beyond doubt. A survey in 1971 showed a density of

T. tubifex and *L. hoffmeisteri* in the area of London Bridge of 300,000 per square metre. A repeat carried out in 1975 by Thames Water Authority biologists revealed a maximum density of only 4,000 per square metre. Further downriver similar decreases in the populations of *T. costatus* and *P. benedeni* were suggested by density comparisons with the 1971 survey. Further evidence of a major decline came from the *Tubifex* 'fishermen', collectors licensed by the Port of London Authority to gather *Tubifex* from the Thames mud for sale as aquaria food. Since early 1975 they have been dismayed by the disappearance of large numbers of the worms from those areas which had provided an abundance in the past. Thames-taken *Tubifex* soon became almost unobtainable in aquaria shops.

That there has been a major change in 'the *Tubifex* population is also suggested by the much lower numbers of wildfowl in recent winters, although this must also be partly due to the mildness of the weather during 1974/75 and 1975/76 which would not have frozen birds off continental waters. A study of bird records on the Inner Thames suggests that the *Tubifex* population may have been gradually changing for a much longer period. There are signs that the decline in *Tubifex* has taken place as the oxygenation of the water has improved progressively from the estuary. The desertion by wildfowl of the sections of the river around Swanscombe, which used to be their stronghold in the early days of their colonisation, can reasonably be attributed to this cause. The 'centre of gravity' of the wildfowl flocks has moved progressively further upriver, and it seems likely that this movement has traced the area of balance between an abundance of *Tubifex* and sufficiently clean conditions to enable the birds to get at it.

Besides the improving oxygenation, another factor probably led to the suddenness of the decline in the *Tubifex* population. Because of very low rainfall during 1974 and 1975, the division between fresh and salt water penetrated much further upriver than normal, and at London Bridge the chloride concentration was as high as 2,000 parts per million in 1975/76 against 100 p.p.m. in 1974/75. In 1975/76 very few tubificids were found in the area of London Bridge of either *T. tubifex* or *L. hoffmeisteri*, and further downstream at Erith *T. costatus* had been replaced by the wholly marine *P. benedeni*.

Such drastic changes in *Tubifex* have obviously been a major factor in the appreciable decline in the numbers of wildfowl in recent winters on the Inner Thames, especially those like pochard and

46

tufted duck which are particularly dependent on this food. Future trends will be closely watched, for it is certain that as the invertebrate fauna of the mudflats change, so will the bird population which they attract. In the 1975/76 winter just passed, there were distinct signs of change already: shovelers, previously extreme rarities on the Inner Thames, were present throughout the winter in the Barking Bay in small numbers, and pochard were present in large flocks in downstream sections of the river where they had not been seen for several winters. It has been suggested that the future may well see flocks of bar-tailed godwits and avocets wintering on the Thames as the habitat and available food alter to suit them. An exciting prospect indeed!

Factors other than those directly connected with the anti-pollution activity have undoubtedly helped the colonisation of the Inner Thames by waders and wildfowl. The great decrease in the amount of shipping using the river in recent years has meant that the tideway is much less disturbed. This would seem to have been a

5: A launch puts up a flock of pochard off Woolwich Arsenal; with the decline of shipping on the Inner Thames the wildfowl are less disturbed.

minor influence, however, for we have noted that the passage of boats causes minimal disturbance to the birds and in some cases large concentrations of both wildfowl and waders use feeding areas close to, or even among, jetties and wharves which are still fully operational. International censuses have shown that the European wintering population of most species of wildfowl has greatly increased in recent years, largely as a result of the long series of mild winters since 1962/63, and because of more effective and widespread conservation: this must clearly have affected the total numbers coming to the Inner Thames. Large numbers of wildfowl have recently been attracted to the new Dutch Ijsselmeer polders, and during cold spells it is likely that at least part of the influxes to the Inner Thames have originated from this area. The availability of an excellent high tide roost site at the ash ponds of the West Thurrock power station since the early 1960's has probably helped waders to take advantage of the improved feeding potential on the adjacent sections of foreshore, although the observed flight-lines of waders feeding on the Inner Thames suggest that a long distance between feeding area and roost site is not a deterrent. While all these factors have contributed to the avian invasion of the Inner Thames,

6. Dunlin flighting in to roost on the ash lagoons at West Thurrock, the site is one of the key factors in drawing waders back to the river.

Diving duck flight into Surrey Docks.

The interior of Abbey Mills Pumping Station.

Detergent pollution.

Oil pollution on the main wader feeding grounds at West Thurrock.

it is clear that none of it could have taken place if the river had remained in its past, grossly polluted state.

It is important to remember that the major part of the colonisation of the Inner Thames has taken place during a remarkably long series of mild winters since 1962/63. Although small peaks in the wildfowl population have occurred during short periods of cold weather during the study period due to influxes from frozen waters locally or on the continent, the potential importance of the Inner Thames as a haven for waders and wildfowl in extremely cold weather has not been fully tested. However the likely effects of such conditions can be judged from the influxes, at that time unprecedented and not equalled until several winters later, which occurred during the arctic conditions of 1962/63, when the Inner Thames was one of the few waters to remain free of ice in northern Europe.

So far we have been mainly concerned with the winter bird population of the Inner Thames. Certainly it is between the end of October and the beginning of March that there is by far the greatest ornithological interest to be found. For during those months the wintering population of waders and wildfowl arrive from their north European breeding grounds and the river becomes alive with birds. In the summer the Inner Thames is relatively birdless, reflecting the unsuitability of the area as a breeding ground for waterfowl. For much of its length the Inner Thames is vertically embanked, and the few remnants of riverside saltings and creeks provide sufficient solitude and calm water for only a few pairs of nesting mallard and one or two pairs of shelduck. In autumn, and to a lesser extent in spring, some riverside marsh areas attract a good variety of migrant wildfowl and waders. Of particular importance in recent years have been the areas used by the Port of London Authority for the disposal of Thames-dredged mud, which is pumped from dredgers by pipeline to huge embanked 'reservoirs'. The resultant lagoons which are created have proved immensely attractive to migrant flocks of waders. Such habitat existed at Swanscombe Marsh in the late 1950's and early 1960's. Later the dredging operations were moved to Rainham Marsh and they still continue there today. Once pumping operations ceased, the lagoons rapidly become overgrown and unsuitable, but at Rainham the lagoons have been operated on a rotational basis, so that ideal conditions for waders are almost permanently available, and the area is undoubtedly the most productive site for migrant waders in the London area if not the whole of south-east England.

Another aspect of the ornithological importance of the Inner Thames may be seen, particularly in autumn, when large numbers of common terns gather around the outflow from the West Thurrock power station. The main attraction is the large numbers of brown shrimps which are caught on the screens of the cooling water intake and passed back to the river through the outflow. This phenomenon is entirely new, and feeding terns were unknown on the Inner Thames during the years of pollution.

The importance of the Inner Thames as a wintering area for wildfowl should not be underestimated. At peak times the total population has approached and probably exceeded the 10,000 mark, the point at which a European wildfowl refuge becomes of prime international importance, as defined by the International Waterfowl Research Bureau. As we have stated, given a severe winter the normally unfrozen waters of the Inner Thames could be crucial to the survival of many more thousands of immigrant duck. A suitable tribute to those involved with the anti-pollution programme was contained in the following recommendation adopted by the International Conference on the Conservation of Wetlands and Waterfowl attended by delegates from thirty-nine countries and ten international organisations which met at Heiligenhafen in West Germany in December 1974:

Recommendation 3, Return of Waterfowl to the Inner Thames in London, England.

The Conference,
NOTING with delight the return of Waterfowl and Fish to the Inner Thames in London, England, as a result of the efforts of the Port of London Authority and the Greater London Council to control pollution in the last decade;
CONGRATULATES the Authorities concerned;
RECOMMENDS to the relevant Authorities of all countries that they take similar steps to reduce pollution of rivers under their control.

CONSERVATION AND THE FUTURE

The dramatic improvements which have been made to the Inner Thames bring new challenges for those concerned with future planning and development along the river. In the past, because of the unhealthy state of the Thames, riverside land could be considered suitable only for the sort of uses which did not bring a large number of people into close contact with the river. Thus there was much industrial building and large areas of land were used for tipping London's rubbish and the dumping of river dredgings.

Now the Thames has been transformed, and it seems essential that full advantage should be taken of its new potential as an area for recreation and housing, so that as many people as possible can benefit from what is undoubtedly a tremendous environmental asset. The birds of the Thames in particular, and its wildlife in general, are an invaluable part of this asset which should be conserved for the enjoyment of all those who come to visit, and live by, the Thames in the future. It would be a disaster if this unique wildlife potential is wasted by future developments which do not take its welfare into account.

There is no reason why, given careful planning and a degree of liaison between planners and wildlife conservationists, all the demands on the Thames should not be met with minimal sacrifices on both sides.

7. This flock of pochard, photographed against a typical dockland backdrop, totalled 4,000 birds.

A major and laudable step in the right direction was taken by the Port of London Authority in November 1974, when it formed its Steering Committee on Conservation and Ecology. The Advisory Panel to this Committee held its first meeting on 10th April, 1975, with representatives from a wide range of national and local organisations interested in wildlife, and a working party is currently producing a report on all aspects of wildlife on the tidal Thames which is due for publication at the end of 1976. It is hoped that this document will enable the PLA (which licenses all works which affect the tidal river, its foreshore and embankments) to assess the effects on wildlife of future developments along the river, and to call on further advice and recommendations from conservationists where necessary.

A further major boost to our efforts at establishing a conservation plan for the Inner Thames involved the Central Electricity Generating Board and its proposals for a new power station on land bordering the long bay on the north side of the river to the east of Barking power stations. In May 1974 we sent a special report to the CEGB, outlining the importance and size of the waterfowl population inhabiting the bay, with suggestions on the siting of both the power station and its fuel delivery jetty in the river and the landscaping of the surrounding land, which would greatly minimise the effect of the development on the birdlife of the Barking Bay.

The CEGB has a well deserved and growing reputation for its enlightened attitude to wildlife conservation on its land, and we were delighted to experience this at first hand on this occasion. In November 1974, we attended a meeting with officials of the CEGB's Planning Department, and we learned that our main suggestions had been incorporated in the final plans for the power station. As a result, when the station is eventually built, it will be set back several hundred yards from the river's edge. The intervening land will be used partly as a public park and partly as a nature reserve, and land alongside the power station will be converted into playing fields. The area proposed for the nature reserve contains a small stream, and with careful management and a selective planting programme the site could become extremely attractive to wildlife.

The fuel delivery jetty will be sited away from the all-important intertidal mudflat which provides the main feeding and roosting area for the wildfowl and waders, so that except during the construction period disturbance to the birdlife will be minimal. Because of the construction of the Thames Barrage the river wall bordering the bay has had to be raised. This work has already been completed, but

8 & 9. Barking Bay with Belvedere Power Station in the distance. This is to be the site of a new power station; but, thanks to consultation with conservationists, the teal in the lower picture should not be banished by the development.

instead of a stark concrete and steel wall which has been used in most other parts of the river, there is now a gently sloping grassed bank which gives a much more pleasant and natural effect to the river bank.

With careful landscaping the impact of the power station itself on the surroundings will be greatly lessened, and an attractive riverside park with nearby sports facilities will be created, in a part of East London which greatly needs this sort of amenity. All this without detriment to the existing birdlife; indeed the attractiveness of the area could be greatly enhanced with an imaginative wildlife management programme in the future.

This is an excellent example of what we believe is the right approach to planning for the Inner Thames. In contrast, two other recent developments have proved disastrous to birdlife on the river, where this need not have been the case if there had been liaison at the planning stage.

The Thames Barrage, now being constructed across the Thames in the Woolwich Reach at Silvertown, is the major component of an essential flood-prevention scheme for London. When completed in the early 1980's, the barrage will be raised from the river bed at

10. The new Thames barrage under construction at Silvertown.

times of surge tides to cut off the flow, thus eliminating the annually increasing risk of extensive flooding in low-lying parts of London.

At the same time it has been necessary to start work on raising the river walls downriver from the barrage site, so that the extra volume of water held back by the barrage can be contained. This has led to the loss of several areas of saltings along the river, by far the most important and extensive of these being the Aveley saltings adjacent to the Rainham Marsh. This area has been destroyed simply because a new river wall was constructed cutting off the 'bay' which contained most of the saltings, instead of raising the height of the existing river wall at the back of the bay.

11 & 12 (overleaf). This before and after sequence shows the loss of tidal foreshore which the new barrage is causing; this site is at Silvertown.

Aveley saltings was not only the one regular nesting site for shelduck in the London area, the only area which attracted numbers of wigeon on the Inner Thames, and a roosting and feeding area for

12.

hundreds of waders and wildfowl, but also the last extensive remnant of this specialised habitat type on the Inner Thames. This area would have been ideal as a nature reserve of immense educational and aesthetic value, but now what could have remained a unique site for wildlife has been ruined and is probably destined for ultimate use as a rubbish tip. The small strip of saltings which remains was still being used by feeding wigeon and roosting waders during the 1975/76 winter, and it is clear that even this much reduced area is still of considerable importance and well worth conserving.

The construction of the new waterfront of Thamesmead on the Erith Marshes near Woolwich has led to the loss of the single most important site for wildfowl on the Inner Thames. The plans for the Thamesmead 'new town' were made before large numbers of wildfowl began visiting the area in the mid-1960's, so the planning authority for this development, the Greater London Council, cannot be blamed for the environmental loss in this case. It does, however, provide an example of the type of development which should be avoided if the Inner Thames is to retain its wealth of wildfowl and waders. The intertidal flats of the long bay between Margaret Ness and Crossness, which used to be the feeding area for up to 5,000 wildfowl and 2,000 waders, are being wholly reclaimed.

Two-thirds of this work is now complete, and the remaining part of the bay (which is still attracting a reduced number of wildfowl and waders in the 1975/76 winter) will gradually disappear when the second phase of construction starts in the near future. It should be made quite clear that our objection does not involve the Thamesmead scheme in itself, which is clearly a much needed part of the GLC's housing programme, but there is no doubt that a revised version of the waterfront design could have retained the present plans for a yachting marina and riverside parkland and also at least part of the existing intertidal area for wildfowl and waders.

The GLC clearly recognises the importance of conserving wildlife in large housing developments for educational and aesthetic purposes, and at Thamesmead several large areas of interesting wildlife habitats have been set aside as nature reserves; a nature trail

13 & 14. Wildfowl at Woolwich Bay before the start of the construction of the new waterfront (overleaf).

14.

and a nature study centre are already in use. It is a great pity that, unless there is an urgent alteration to the plans for the second phase of the Thamesmead waterfront, which now seems unlikely despite our efforts to achieve this, the wildfowl and waders will be ousted from the area entirely. They could have formed a unique addition to the nature study potential already existing, but instead the Thamesmead waterfront seems doomed to a future of sterile concrete completely devoid of wildlife. It seems ironic that several hundred pounds have been spent on stocking the ornamental lake at Thamesmead with a collection of wing-clipped and bread-begging exotic wildfowl, while vast flocks of colourful waterbirds have been driven away from the area by development which did not take their welfare into account.

In an enclosed waterway such as the Inner Thames the potential dangers of oil spills are particularly acute to the wildfowl and waders. The responsibility of dealing with oil pollution in the river remains with the Port of London Authority, whereas all other pollution control responsibility was passed to the Thames Water Authority on its formation in April 1974. In our experience the past handling of oil spills by the PLA has been exemplary.

15 & 16. A few wing-clipped waterfowl on ornamental lakes will not compensate the new town of Thamesmead for scenes like these.

In one case we discovered oil leaking into the river from storage tanks at West Thurrock, in January 1974, and we were pleasantly surprised to find a PLA team already on their way to deal with it even before we had had a chance to report the spillage ourselves. About a mile of shore was polluted between West Thurrock and Purfleet, a major feeding area for waders, but during the next few days we found a total of only five dead dunlin and redshank, a surprisingly small mortality due largely to the prompt handling of the situation. The fact that the company at fault on this occasion was fined £5,000 is some measure of the seriousness with which oil pollution is treated on the Inner Thames, which is a very welcome situation.

Past experience clearly illustrates the need for closer cooperation between the planners and wildlife conservationists if the Inner Thames is to retain its bird population for the benefit of future generations. With the formation of the Port of London Authority's Steering Committee on Conservation and Ecology there is every opportunity for expert advice to be sought on all facets of wildlife on the Thames, so that this can be taken into account in all

17. *Envoi!* An escort of teal for the *Carolina*.

developments which affect the tidal river and foreshore, and the riverside areas of open ground. The story of the return of a profusion of wildfowl and waders to the Inner Thames is one of a wildlife triumph against seemingly insuperable odds. It is an achievement unique in the world, of which Britain can feel justly proud. We hope it will not be wasted.

CHAPTER 3

THE WILDFOWL

❧

THE systematic lists for the Inner Thames in the two following chapters cover the period from 1900 to the end of the 1975/76 winter. This means that, where relevant, the past status of species can be compared with results during our main study period from 1960 to 1975/76 when the large influxes occurred. Particular attention is paid to the status of birds on the river itself, for it is here that the main effects of the anti-pollution campaign have been felt. Where relevant, results are compared with the situation elsewhere in the London area and further afield. The marshes bordering the Inner Thames are important to many species of waterbirds, and their status in these areas is also summarised.

To simplify the counting and evaluation of wildfowl and wader flocks, the Inner Thames has been divided into sections (Figure 3). In many cases tables have been used as a more convenient way of displaying the data: these in most examples contain a 'Minimum Total' figure, and this gives the minimum peak population of the whole Inner Thames at any one time, based on simultaneous counts in different parts of the river or counts of large single concentrations. It should be borne in mind that this figure is obviously very much less than the actual number of birds using the Inner Thames during the course of a winter, as passage or transitory flocks are very often not included.

Mute Swan

For centuries the mute swan has been one of the most familiar birds of the Upper Thames. Some idea of their abundance on the river can be gained from the records of the numbers marked annually during the ancient and picturesque ceremony of swan-upping, in which birds are caught and bill-marked for the Crown and the the Livery

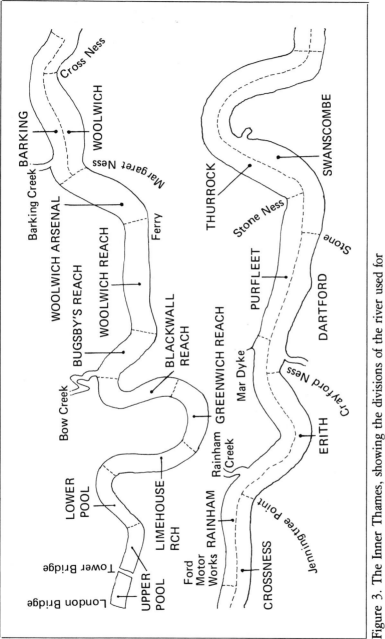

Figure 3. The Inner Thames, showing the divisions of the river used for counts. The site names correspond with those in the text and tables.

Companies of the City of London. Swan-upping takes place each July, formerly on the thirty-mile section between Staines and Battersea bridges, but since the 1940's only the twenty-seven-mile section from Staines to Putney Bridge has been covered.

The number marked each year shows a steady increase from the beginning of the present century up to a peak of 418 in 1938. Subsequently numbers were lower, but counts from other sources show that a generally high population continues to inhabit the Upper Thames. The most striking evidence of this came as a result of the sinking of an oil barge at Battersea in 1956, which resulted in a total of 803 contaminated birds being collected by the RSPCA and the PDSA, of which 243 are known to have died.

In contrast to their abundance on the reaches through and above London, however, they were almost a rarity on the polluted reaches below London. The largest flock seen by John F. Burton during his studies of the river from Greenwich to Tilbury between 1945 and 1950 was one of nine at Swanscombe in November 1950, and this dearth of mute swans on the Inner Thames is confirmed by the otherwise complete lack of records up to the 1960's.

The first indication of the subsequent massive increases on the Inner Thames was the presence of a flock of up to 71 around Bow Creek in Bugsby's Reach during the 1968/69 winter, coinciding with the first arrival of large numbers of other species. In the following winter there were up to 185 at Woolwich and 200 at Crossness. By 1970/71 the flock at Bow Creek had increased to 300.

By 1973 mute swans were well established on the Inner Thames, with the main concentrations in Bugsby's and Woolwich reaches, but large flocks also occurred at Barking and Crossness: the table summarises the main counts for that year at these sites, together with complete or part counts which show the minimum population for the Inner Thames.

Table 1: *Main counts of mute swans on the Inner Thames during 1973*

	Jan	Feb	Mar	Apr	May	Jun	Jul	Aug	Sep	Oct	Nov	Dec
Bugsby's Reach	—	—	—	—	210	216	—	467	—	—	—	220
Woolwich Reach	377	—	219	130	—	262	—	—	331	—	—	105
Barking	—	—	—	120	—	—	—	—	—	—	—	—
Crossness	—	—	—	—	132	120	100	—	—	—	—	—
Total Inner Thames	420	—	227	260	406	616	100	587	343	—	—	220

wn shrimps and young flatfish from the filter screens at West Thurrock Power Station.

ehouses being demolished at Surrey Docks and (inset) a little ringed plover's nest
d the debris.

18. Spillage from the grain wharves at Silvertown is an attraction for this herd of mute swans.

The largest concentrations now occur annually during the summer months when numbers are boosted by the arrival of non-breeding adults. The count of 616 on 27th June, 1973 is the highest yet recorded on the Inner Thames, which now boasts one of the largest concentrations of mute swans anywhere in Britain. This represents a remarkable change in status within only ten years, although a series of reports during the early 1960's of declining numbers on the upper Thames suggests a downriver shift of a large part of the population, rather than the recruitment of new birds from further afield. It would seem that while numbers on the Inner Thames have increased dramatically, the population of the Thames as a whole has probably not changed a great deal. Recoveries of ringed birds have shown that the congregations on the Thames are entirely drawn from breeding areas in London and its environs, and it seems likely that the major factor controlling the size of the population is the availability of suitable nesting waters. For many years the large number of non-breeding adults present on the Thames during the breeding season has suggested an excess over the number of available breeding sites in the London area.

Until 1975 the main focal point for the Inner Thames mute swan herds was the Union Mills Wharf at Silvertown, where spillages of grain, soya beans, peanuts etc. being unloaded from barges provide a

65

major food source. The availability of a secluded 'loafing' area in the adjacent Bow Creek is undoubtedly an additional attraction. This wharf closed in 1975, however, and now the main congregations are found in the area of the Mollassine Wharf at Greenwich. It is tempting to suggest that the cleaner condition of the river is entirely responsible for the birds' new presence there, enabling them to take advantage of a food supply which has always been available. However, we have also seen them taking the green algae, *Enteromorpha sp.*, which have become increasingly prolific on the banks and pilings in recent years as a direct result of the more oxygenated water, and also *Tubifex* worms. These items clearly augment their diet at times when there are no barges unloading, and then they visit other parts of the Inner Thames where these alternatives provide a continuity of food supply without which they might not be able to exist.

Shelduck

The cleaner Thames has dramatically changed the status of shelduck in London. Until the 1960's, and particularly since 1930, it was considered a very scarce and irregular visitor, occurring mainly on the reservoirs near the Thames in west London. Flocks of more than ten were extremely rare and the pattern of records had peaks in the spring and autumn, which contrasts with their present status as mainly winter visitors. Since 1960 shelduck are seen much more frequently in the London area, and flocks of more than ten occur almost annually now, and this improved situation is clearly connected with the large numbers now found on the Inner Thames.

The colonisation of the Inner Thames started earlier than most of the other species involved. Before the 1950's it had been virtually unknown between London and Tilbury, but during that decade small numbers were seen regularly. This was before the anti-pollution activity had started, so this initial influx was the result of a genuine range expansion. Parties of up to ten frequented the riverside marshes at Swanscombe, Dartford and Rainham. In 1954 a pair bred at Aveley saltings, the first time that shelduck had nested in London, and since 1959 a total of up to three pairs have nested annually at these three sites. Nowadays the only regular nesting area in London is the Aveley saltings, but work on realigning the sea wall which started there in the summer of 1975 may well have been the cause of their failure to nest there in that year. Instead, two pairs nested on rough ground near the Beckton sewage works about five

19. Shelduck moving upriver at Crossness.

miles upriver, and it seems likely that these were the birds displaced from Aveley.

The quite separate massive increase in the wintering population, which gained pace from the early 1960's, is best shown by a table of peak counts since the winter of 1960/61 (Table 2). The first large numbers were seen in the severe winter of 1962/63, and numbers remained high for the next five winters. Between 1968/69 and 1971/72 the winter influxes reached invasion proportions, and a gradual upriver shift began which is still continuing.

As with so many species on the Thames, the Shelduck has suffered from habitat destruction in the Woolwich bay and in the Woolwich Reach at Silvertown, resulting from the Thamesmead and Thames Barrage projects respectively. Fortunately they seem adaptable to other sites, so overall numbers may not be drastically reduced as will undoubtedly be the case with more specialised species. They like the bay at Barking in particular, and this site provided the largest flocks in the last three winters, so the concern

Table 2 : *Peak counts of shelduck at sites on the Inner Thames, 1960/61 to 1975/76*

	Upper Pool to Greenwich Reach	Limehouse Reach	Blackwall Reach	Bugsby's Reach	Woolwich Reach	Woolwich Arsenal	Woolwich	Barking	Crossness	Rainham	Erith	Dartford	Purfleet	Swanscombe	Thurrock	MINIMUM TOTAL
1960/61	—	—	—	—	—	—	—	—	—	15	—	—	—	7	—	15
1961/62	—	—	—	—	—	—	—	—	—	24	—	—	—	72	—	72
1962/63	—	—	—	—	—	—	—	—	—	30	—	85	—	500	—	500
1963/64	—	—	—	—	—	—	—	—	—	13	—	—	—	226	—	226
1964/65	—	—	—	—	—	—	—	—	—	43	—	600	—	—	—	600
1965/66	—	—	—	—	—	—	—	—	—	59	—	—	—	120	—	120
1966/67	—	—	—	—	—	—	—	—	—	58	—	—	—	150	—	150
1967/68	—	—	—	—	—	—	—	—	—	157	—	140	150	250	—	250
1968/69	—	—	—	—	—	—	1000	—	—	550	—	—	—	1000	—	1000
1969/70	—	—	—	—	—	—	1600	—	—	1000	—	1000	—	1500	—	3000
1970/71	—	—	—	—	—	10	600	43	75	900	600	800	200	1500	—	1500
1971/72	—	—	—	—	—	—	731	800	154	850	520	1000	880	1500	1000	2600
1972/73	—	—	35	—	—	60	142	197	105	590	150	100	215	303	18	929
1973/74	—	—	—	—	500	—	500	682	250	510	50	—	—	100	—	868
1974/75	—	—	—	—	—	50	265	380	245	130	—	—	50	8	—	629
1975/76	—	2	—	—	218	67	181	484	—	26	—	—	282	14	—	932

shown by the CEGB over the siting of a new power station there is especially welcome as far as the future presence of shelduck on the Thames is concerned.

Wigeon

The wigeon is by far the most specialised and local of all the wildfowl which regularly winter on the Inner Thames. Records are almost entirely confined to the flock which frequents the area of grass-covered saltings which border the river at Aveley on the Rainham marshes. This is the only site on the Inner Thames which contains an extensive area of short-cropped grass, and provides one of the preferred feeding habitats of the species. This type of habitat has probably not been greatly affected by the clean up of the river, and this combined with the lack of other suitable sites explains why wigeon have not shown the dramatic increases of some other species of wildfowl in the last decade.

Between 1945 and 1950 John F. Burton and others recorded wigeon regularly on this part of the river and at Swanscombe in numbers up to thirty, and this level of numbers seems to have been maintained up to the mid-1960's apart from an exceptional flock of 180 at Aveley in the severe 1962/63 winter. Winter counts of the flock based at Aveley are given below (Table 3). These birds occasionally visit adjacent sections of the river at Erith and Dartford and probably account for two flocks seen a little further afield at Swanscombe (160 in December 1970 and nineteen in January 1973); certainly we are not aware of any other regular *feeding* site for wigeon other than Aveley in recent years.

Table 3: *Peak winter counts of wigeon at Aveley saltings, 1968/69 to 1975/76*

1968/69	1969/70	1970/71	1971/72	1972/73	1973/74	1974/75	1975/76
200	150	200	65	100	25	26	41

Certainly the average for wigeon has increased since the 1940's and 1950's, but with the probability that the habitat at Aveley has changed little over the same period it seems more likely that this is connected with the marked increases noted for wigeon further out in the estuary on the North Kent Marshes. The low counts in 1973/74 and 1974/75 are probably a result of the mildness of the winters.

Wigeon arrive late in the year at Aveley, and peak numbers are not reached until January or February. This suggests a further connection with the population of the North Kent Marshes where a change of feeding habitat is noted around this time of year, from the intertidal flats to grassy brackish marshes akin to the habitat at Aveley.

Work associated with the construction of the Thames Barrage began at Aveley in the summer of 1975. It involved raising and realigning the sea wall and although only a small strip of undisturbed saltings remains, the effect seems to have been minimal, and the usual wintering flock of wigeon returned in the 1975/76 winter.

Teal

The records which are available for the first half of the present century suggest that teal were fairly frequent in late autumn and

Table 4: *Peak winter counts of teal at sites on the Inner Thames, 1961/62 to 1975/76*

	Upper Pool to Woolwich Reach	Woolwich Arsenal	Woolwich	Barking	Crossness	Rainham‡	Erith	Dartford	Purfleet	Swanscombe	Thurrock	MINIMUM TOTAL
1961/62	—	—	—	—	—	—	—	—	—	250	—	250
1962/63	—	—	—	250	—	—	—	—	—	500	—	500
1963/64	—	—	—	173	—	—	—	—	—	—	—	173
1964/65	—	—	—	—	—	—	—	—	—	—	—	—
1965/66	—	—	400	—	—	—	—	—	—	—	—	400
1966/67	—	—	—	—	—	—	—	—	—	—	—	—
1967/68	—	—	—	—	—	—	—	—	—	—	—	—
1968/69	—	—	450	—	—	200	—	—	—	—	—	450
1969/70	—	—	800	—	—	1000	—	—	—	—	—	1000
1970/71	—	—(.. 1500 total ..)				300	—	—	—	100*	—	1500
1971/72	—	—	400	630	6	100	—	—	—	—	—	730
1972/73	—	—	1720	800	1	40	—	107†	—	—	—	800
1973/74	—	—	—	800	—	250	—	—	—	—	—	800
1974/75	—	—	56	410	—	95	—	—	—	—	—	430
1975/76	—	38	3	182	6	650	—	—	2	—	—	650

* Flock flying west 27th December, 1970.
† Flock flying west 26th January, 1973.
‡ Mainly on Rainham Marsh rather than the river itself.

20. Teal low over the mud at Barking Bay.

winter on the lower reaches of the Inner Thames. Numbers were very small by present day standards, however, and in summarising a series of records between 1945 and 1950 John F. Burton found that flocks greater than twenty were rare and parties between four and ten were more usual. In hard winters they were more frequent and penetrated as far upriver as Crossness. The largest flock seen during this period was fifty-five at Swanscombe in December 1949. This background gives perspective to the remarkable increases which have taken place since 1960 summarised in the Table.

The high counts at the beginning of the decade from Swanscombe and Barking were largely the result of cold weather which had driven the birds to the river from frozen waters elsewhere, and they gave the first signs that the condition of the river was improving sufficiently to support a sizeable population of teal. The count of 400 in the Woolwich bay in 1965/66 was remarkable as it was the first time this upriver site had been occupied and more significantly it occurred during a mild winter. After that the Woolwich, Barking and Rainham sections became the strongholds for the species on the Inner Thames. Teal have not shown adaptability to new sites to the same extent as most other species, suggesting that their habitat requirements may be more specialised. The reclamation of most of the mudflats in the Woolwich bay during 1973 cut numbers there drastically, and if present proposals are followed through, the whole of the mudflat will disappear. Fortunately the alternative site at Barking on the other side of the river is available, and surprisingly the total population of the area does not seem to have been seriously affected, although the amount of subsequent data is small. In recent years numbers of teal have been rather less than usual on the river at Rainham, and with the bay at Woolwich under threat of complete destruction the mudflats at Barking become of crucial importance to the future presence of teal on the Inner Thames. Cold weather locally or on the continent invariably results in larger numbers of teal appearing on the Inner Thames, and the lower counts in latter part of the study period must largely reflect the comparative mildness of the winters.

For many years teal have been regular and quite numerous visitors to the London reservoirs. The average total winter population for these sites has been decreasing steadily from 1,157 in 1969/70 to 605 in 1973/74. As on the Thames much of this decrease is probably due to the mild winters, but the increasing attractiveness of the Inner Thames may also have had an effect by drawing birds from these more traditional areas. Certainly, however, a study of the reservoir figures and the peak counts on the Thames show that the effect of this, if any, has not been very great, and overall there has been a significant increase in the total of teal now wintering in the London area as a whole.

Tubifex is the main food of teal when they are feeding on the mud flats of the river itself, but large numbers gather from time to time on Rainham Marshes, especially on the flooded beds of seeding sea aster which has overgrown some of the dredged mud reservoirs. When feeding on the mudflats they tend to range more widely over the exposed mud at low tide than other species, sometimes feeding a great distance from the edge of the water right under the river wall. This habit may be the reason for their choice of the wider mudflats on the Inner Thames, which are available in the Barking and Woolwich sections.

72

THE WILDFOWL

Mallard

Although the mallard has always been abundant and widespread in the London area, its vastly increased numbers on the Inner Thames as a result of the cleaner conditions form a no less important and significant part of the story.

On the Thames above London it has always been a familiar bird of the river, and at times extremely abundant especially in winter. Regular counts between Putney and Teddington during the 1950's and 1960's showed that the total in this section regularly exceeded 1,000 birds during the winter, and in times of severely cold weather some astonishingly high totals were reached, such as 3,630 in January 1963: even the urbanised reaches through the heart of London are rarely without mallard, and in the same hard winter there were as many as sixty in the half-mile section between Southwark and Blackfriars bridges.

Up to the late 1960's, however, its status on the Inner Thames

21. Mallard against an incongruous skyline.

downriver from London was one of extreme scarcity by present-day standards. It is surely a most significant indicator of the high degree of pollution which existed in the river when one considers that even mallard, a completely ubiquitous species elsewhere in London showing great tolerance of human disturbance and urbanisation, should almost completely shun the whole of the London to Tilbury river because of the foul conditions which existed. Writing of the period between 1945 and 1950 during the worst pollution, John F. Burton described the mallard as being not often found on the river between London and Gravesend, and the few which frequented the Greenwich and Blackwall reaches were from the ornamental pond in nearby Greenwich Park. Jeremy Brock, who studied the birds of the Rainham area between 1960 and 1964, never saw more than thirty on that section of the river, and none at all on the Woolwich and Barking sections between 1960 and 1966. Those birds which did frequent the river probably fed on grain spilled in and around the docks and wharves rather than a natural food supply: this is suggested by the discovery of wheat grains in the gizzards of mallard shot flighting to St James's Park between 1944 and 1945, and our own observations show that some still take advantage of this food source.

It is surprising that the first records of large flocks on the Inner Thames did not occur until 1968/69, rather later than is evident for other species of wildfowl. However it seems likely that the initial stages of the colonisation passed unrecorded, for with such a familiar bird it would take exceptional numbers to attract the attention of most ornithologists. Be that as it may, the presence of up to 500 in the Woolwich section and over 100 at both Barking and Rainham in the winter of 1968/69 represented a dramatic transformation by any standards, considering that only four or five winters previously Jeremy Brock had seen none in the first two sites and only up to thirty in the other. Since then there has been a marked increase in numbers and a spread to other sites, the latter trend especially evident since the 1970/71 winter. The overall picture is shown by the table which gives the peak winter count for each site along the Inner Thames.

Several factors suggest that the winter flocks of mallard are of relatively local origin, in contrast to other species of wildfowl and waders which come in the main from continental breeding areas. Counts do not show, for example, the fluctuations associated with cold weather influxes from the continent as is evident for other species. Also there has been a drop in numbers on the Thames

Table 5: *Peak winter counts of Mallard at sites on the Inner Thames, 1967/68 to 1975/76*

	Upper Pool	Lower Pool	Limehouse Reach	Greenwich Reach	Blackwall Reach	Bugsby's Reach	Woolwich Reach	Woolwich Arsenal	Woolwich	Barking	Crossness	Rainham	Erith	Dartford	Purfleet	Swanscombe	Thurrock	MINIMUM TOTAL
1967/68	—	—	—	—	—	—	—	—	—	—	—	—	—	—	—	—	—	—
1968/69	—	—	—	—	—	—	—	—	500	120	—	—	—	—	—	—	—	500
1969/70	—	—	—	—	—	—	—	—	700	—	—	107	—	—	—	—	—	700
1970/71	—	—	—	—	—	—	—	30	750	180	—	41	45	—	75	—	60	900
1971/72	(	··········	50 total	)	18	50	113	610	500	326	100	71	10	14	12	10	17	1174
1972/73	20	14	—	—	64	156	276	615	900	293	400	200	—	8	8	12	67	1490
1973/74	96	20	102	4	55	150	200	342	180	659	225	59	3	—	2	—	—	1445
1974/75	94	70	120	30	—	—	—	450	110	590	180	60	45	—	—	—	—	1300
1975/76	45	12	35	—	149	237	196	467	65	193	187	110	208	—	13	—	—	1179

75

22. The wharves on the Inner Thames are a favourite resting place for mallard.

above London in recent years, corresponding with the increases below London. This suggests that the same basic population has been involved in a downriver shift to take advantage of the cleaner conditions. This fact probably explains why the initial influxes did not start in the lower reaches around Swanscombe and Dartford, a pattern which has typified the colonisation of the Inner Thames by species which have originated from the continent.

Because the counts of mallard have been relatively unaffected by weather conditions abroad, they are probably a more accurate barometer of the improving condition of the Thames than is the case with counts of other species. With this in mind it is encouraging to note the steady increase which has taken place. Even in the exceptionally mild winter of 1974/75 counts were well up to average.

The habitat requirements of mallard on the Inner Thames are fairly unspecialised, as indicated by their occupation of many sections of the river not frequented by other species. Thus they will probably be less affected by future developments and habitat changes. However the destruction of the mudflats in the Woolwich

76

bay by the extension of the waterfront of the Thamesmead 'new town' severely reduced numbers there after 1972/73, showing that there is a limit to the amount of disturbance that even mallard will tolerate. Clearly we should not be complacent about the certainty of the presence of large numbers on the Thames in the future.

The mallard is the only species of duck which nests regularly in fair numbers on the Inner Thames (in fact the only other species is shelduck with up to three pairs annually). Even so our observations suggest that the number of pairs on the river itself in the whole twenty-five miles from London to Tilbury is pitifully small, and probably does not regularly exceed about ten. While the Inner Thames may be a haven for wintering flocks of wildfowl, it is clearly a most hostile environment for breeding. Those which do nest use the creeks and saltings which provide greater seclusion, and at times bizarre situations such as moored barges and nest sites on riverside constructions often high above the water. Duckling survival must be minimal as a result of the fast tidal flow and the vertical embankments which offer little protection. However, many pairs nest on the riverside marshes, ponds and gravel pits, and although there are no figures to prove it, the breeding population of these areas has probably increased as a result of the good feeding areas now provided by the river which has attracted many more adults to the general area during the summer. Certainly quite large flocks of drake mallard are a feature of the Thames in the summer months, although these could well be unmated birds.

As with other wildfowl on the Thames the main food of mallard is *Tubifex* worms. However, especially during the summer months, we have often seen them feeding on the green algae, *Enteromorpha*, which have become increasingly prolific on the banks and pilings in recent years as a direct result of the cleaner conditions. Mute swans, coot and moorhens are the only other species which we have seen taking advantage of this food source on the Inner Thames. Grain spillages around the wharves also form an important part of the diet for some of the population.

Pintail

The status of the pintail in the London area has been completely transformed as a result of the clean up of the Thames. Until the 1960's it used to be an extremely infrequent visitor in very small numbers. The largest flock ever recorded was twenty-six on the Walton reservoirs in West London during the severe winter of

23. Pintail and a mallard duck (second from right) 'tubifexing'.

1946/47, otherwise more than ten had ever been seen together. On the Thames there were fifteen between Putney and Richmond in the same winter which were probably some of the Walton birds, but apart from these there have only been about ten records since the beginning of the century, involving never more than four birds at a time.

On the Inner Thames between London and Tilbury, pintail were not recorded at all until 1954 when there were three at Rainham on 30th January, but between 1960 and 1968 they began to occur with increasing frequency with a series of records from Swanscombe, Dartford and Rainham. The highest numbers during this period were twenty-three in 1962/63 and sixty in 1967/68, both at Rainham, but even then they frequented the riverside 'marshes' rather than the tidal mud of the river itself.

It was in the following winter of 1968/69 that this habitat was used by large numbers for the first time, with up to 20 at Swanscombe and no less than 130 in the bay in the Woolwich

Table 6: Peak winter counts of pintail at sites on the Inner Thames, 1965/66 to 1975/76

	Upper Pool to Greenwich Reach	Blackwall Reach	Bugsby's Reach	Woolwich Reach	Woolwich Arsenal	Woolwich	Barking	Crossness	Rainham	Erith	Dartford	Purfleet	Swanscombe	Thurrock	MINIMUM TOTAL
1965/66	—	—	—	—	—	—	—	—	—	—	—	—	—	—	—
1966/67	—	—	—	—	—	—	—	—	1*	—	—	—	—	—	1*
1967/68	—	—	—	—	—	—	—	6*	60*	—	100†	—	20	—	60*
1968/69	—	—	—	—	—	130	—	—	12*	—	—	—	—	—	130
1969/70	—	—	—	—	—	350	—	—	70*	—	—	—	—	—	350
1970/71	—	—	—	—	—	200	27	95	—	10	—	55	26†	100	367
1971/72	—	—	—	—	—	275	95	101	26	—	—	25	—	—	275
1972/73	—	1	—	3	29	(......485 total......)		40	—	19	20	28	—	485
1973/74	—	35	2	75	10	150	18	140	—	15	6	1	27	—	231
1974/75	—	6	—	—	1	175	50	26	150*	15	—	—	—	—	196
1975/76	—	—	—	15	48	10	—	2	12	—	—	—	—	—	70

* Mainly on riverside marshes rather than the river itself.
† Seen in flight only.

79

section, by far the largest flock ever recorded in the London area up to that time. In the subsequent four winters they became more established, spreading to new sites on the river and increasing in numbers to a peak total population of 485 in 1972/73. The table shows clearly this remarkable increase and expansion of range up to 1972/73, but since then these trends have been adversely affected by two major setbacks. Firstly the favourite area for pintail, the bay at Woolwich, was largely built over during the extension of the waterfront as part of the Thamesmead 'new town' scheme. Fortunately a small section of the bay still remains unspoiled, and continues to attract good numbers, but this too is destined for ultimate development. Part of this population was driven elsewhere, some to a new area at Silvertown in the Woolwich Reach, where there were up to seventy-five during the 1973/74 winter. Secondly, during 1974, the new feeding area at Silvertown was rendered unsuitable by work on the construction of the Thames Barrage. The overall effect of these two setbacks has been to greatly reduce the numbers of pintail in recent winters, and with the impending destruction of what remains of the Woolwich bay the future for this species does not look bright. It can only be hoped they will move into new areas, and the sites at Barking, Crossness and Rainham are perhaps the most likely as they have all held large numbers in the past.

Records suggest that the pintail populations of the Inner Thames, the North Kent Marshes and the Essex marshes are all closely connected. Decreases at one or more of these areas have often coincided with increases at the other. This is particularly true of the initial influxes into the Inner Thames during the late 1960's and early 1970's which coincided with corresponding drops in the Essex and Kent estuarine populations, and there are actual observations of flocks moving west upriver from these areas towards the Inner Thames. Flocks begin to arrive at the end of September, gradually building to a peak in normal winters towards the end of December. Spring departure takes place during March, although recently some stragglers have remained into May.

The main food of pintail on the Inner Thames is *Tubifex* worms which they obtain either by upending in shallow water in the manner typical of the species, or by probing vigorously in the wet exposed mud, never far from the receding tide. At Rainham in particular large numbers sometimes flight to the grazing marsh and the overgrown dredged mud 'reservoirs' to feed, and 155 were present there in January 1975.

The addition of large numbers of pintail to the avifauna of London as a direct result of the cleaner Thames is one of the most pleasant aspects of the anti-pollution programme. Already their numbers have suffered as a result of developments along the river. It would be a major asset of future conservation work if these elegant duck can continue to grace the Thames. It would be a great pity if future developments do not take their welfare into account and they once again become a great rarity in London.

Pochard

At the beginning of this century the pochard was rather scarce in London. Small flocks, rarely exceeding a hundred, used to occur on such waters as the lake in Richmond Park, or Barn Elms reservoir. A general increase began in the 1930's, and was accelerated by the construction of the larger reservoirs.

Before the clean-up, large numbers were virtually unknown anywhere on the Thames, except in very cold weather when it provided the only unfrozen water. Such conditions produced a flock of 1,000 in the Wandsworth area in 1947 and seventy between Barn Elms and Richmond in 1962/63. On the reaches below London, however, it has been virtually unknown since the beginning of the century.

24. Pochard photographed over the bows of the launch.

The first signs that the situation was changing came in the 1961/62 winter when flocks of up to 175 came into both the Rainham and Swanscombe sections, and in the following winter when there were up to 500 at Swanscombe. At the time the main factor for these unprecedented numbers was thought to be the cold weather, but it is now clear that the first effects of the cleaner river were being felt. Numbers on the Inner Thames did not again exceed a hundred until the winter of 1968/69, when large numbers moved into the Woolwich bay and the flock built up to an astonishing 1,500 during a period of mild weather.

The subsequent increase and spread upriver is best shown by the table of peak counts for each site on the Inner Thames.

The highest count has been 4,000 in the 1971/72 winter, by far the largest flock anywhere in the London area. In the following two winters numbers were lower largely due to the mild weather, a situation not helped by the destruction of the pochards' favourite feeding area at Woolwich as part of the Thamesmead scheme. The reclamation of the mudflat there was largely complete by the 1973/74 winter, and accounts for the massive drop in numbers at this site: the major upriver spread in the same winter was largely the result of displaced birds seeking new feeding areas.

The further drastic drop in numbers in the last two winters is presumably the combined effect of several factors, most important of which is the decline of *Tubifex* worms which has provided their almost exclusive food on the Inner Thames. It is interesting that the largest flock in the 1975/76 winter was at Erith, a downriver section which has not held large numbers since 1970. It is possible that these pochard were feeding on a different species of *Tubifex* or some other invertebrate which has recently colonised that part of the river.

Observations of flight lines showed that the Thames pochard flight from the river, especially in rough weather, to roost on the more secluded waters of the nearby reservoirs. Those at Stoke Newington and Walthamstow in particular have benefitted, and when numbers have been high on the Thames, flocks in excess of 1,000 were regularly recorded there. In the winter of 1970/71 up to 1,700 pochard roosted in the disused Surrey Docks. Clearly the availability of secluded roosting areas has been an important factor in attracting pochard to the Thames.

In common with many other species on the Thames, *Tubifex* is the main food of the pochard. This is remarkable as this is the first time that they have been known to take this food, and they do so on

82

Table 7: Peak winter counts of pochard at sites on the Inner Thames, 1966/67 to 1975/76

	Upper Pool	Lower Pool	Limehouse Reach	Greenwich Reach	Blackwall Reach	Bugsby's Reach	Woolwich Reach	Woolwich Arsenal	Woolwich	Barking	Crossness	Rainham	Erith	Dartford to Thurrock	MINIMUM TOTAL
1966/67	—	—	—	—	—	—	—	—	—	—	—	—	—	—	—
1967/68	—	—	—	—	—	—	—	—	—	—	—	—	100	—	100
1968/69	—	—	—	—	—	—	—	—	1500	—	—	—	—	—	1500
1969/70	—	—	—	—	—	—	—	—	2500	—	—	35	—	—	2500
1970/71	—	—	—	—	—	—	35	523	2000	400	52	100	190	—	2000
1971/72	30	450	—	—	4	25	465	600	4000	1500	468	131	—	3	4000
1972/73	310	400	1250	—	200	—	1050	60	2500	2600	550	1080	—	23	2600
1973/74	—	—	500	—	—	—	83	1	88	200	165	—	31	—	2471
1974/75	—	—	—	—	—	—	—	1	370	420	—	—	—	—	581
1975/76	—	—	—	—	—	—	110	—	—	4	—	—	175	—	175

the Thames apparently to the exclusion of anything else. Perhaps more surprising is the fact that they seem to have changed their feeding habits to take advantage of this food source. Pochard normally dive below the surface to take food, and while they mostly do so to get at the *Tubifex*, we have also seen them probing for it in the exposed mud in the manner of dabbling duck, which seems to be an entirely new method of feeding for this species. It is amusing to see their reactions when left on the mud by the ebbing tide, for they suddenly seem to realise that as good diving duck, this is quite wrong and with one accord they run in a most ungainly fashion back to the water's edge and start probing again!

The invasion of the Thames by large numbers of these colourful duck from north European breeding grounds has been a spectacular part of the Thames wildlife story. National surveys have shown that at peak times the river has held up to six per cent of the total British population, a remarkable figure for an area where prior to 1968 the occurrence of pochard had been considered remarkable.

Tufted Duck

The past and present status of tufted duck in the London area as a whole is very similar to that of pochard. It was comparatively scarce

25. A foggy morning at Surrey Docks; a roost for tufted duck and pochard from the river.

Table 8: Peak winter counts of tufted duck at sites on the Inner Thames, 1967/68 to 1975/76

	Upper Pool	Lower Pool	Limehouse Reach	Greenwich Reach	Blackwall Reach	Bugsby's Reach	Woolwich Reach	Woolwich Arsenal	Woolwich	Barking	Crossness	Rainham	Erith	Dartford to Thurrock	MINIMUM TOTAL
1967/68	—	—	—	—	—	—	—	—	—	—	—	—	—	—	—
1968/69	—	—	—	—	—	—	—	—	400	—	—	—	—	—	400
1969/70	—	—	—	—	—	—	—	—	800	—	—	104	—	—	800
1970/71	—	—	—	—	—	—	—	—	400	—	—	20	—	—	400
1971/72	—	—	—	—	—	—	—	2	450	100	10	42	2	—	458
1972/73	—	—	—	—	—	10	69	4	210	13	300	44	30	—	300
1973/74	40	25	50	—	—	—	50	2	30	11	200	—	—	—	200
1974/75	3	—	200	—	—	—	14	1	7	—	—	—	—	—	200
1975/76	2	—	—	—	—	—	77	—	—	—	—	—	20	—	81

85

at the beginning of the present century, but numbers have steadily increased to the present abundance in winter, due largely to the availability of expanses of water provided by the newly constructed reservoirs. Their numbers have increased even more than pochard, and by the late 1960's tufted duck had taken over from mallard as London's most abundant species of wildfowl in winter. Counts on London's main wildfowl waters (not including the Inner Thames) show that since 1969/70 the average winter population has exceeded that of mallard, with the mean of the five winters from 1969/70 to 1973/74 at 4,538 compared with 3,027 for mallard.

These dramatic increases have not been reflected in their numbers on the Inner Thames, where they have been much less numerous than pochard, and clearly the riverine habitat is not so attractive to tufted duck.

While the numbers which have colonised the Inner Thames have not been as great as for pochard, the pattern of their increase and spread has been very similar as shown in the table, and they have always shown a close association with the pochard flocks.

Scaup

Until the late 1960's scaup were scarce anywhere on the Thames, and only during very cold weather were more than five seen together. In 1946/47, for example, there were several flocks of up to twenty-six on the upper Thames between Wandsworth and Kew bridges, and in 1962/63 there was a gathering of more than a hundred at Dartford.

The latter is by far the largest number ever seen on the Thames, and as well as the arctic weather conditions at the time it seems likely that the cleaner conditions which were then beginning to prevail were a contributory factor.

Since 1968/69, scaup have been of annual occurrence on the Inner Thames, and in significantly higher numbers than before although they have not shown the dramatic increases of other species. They are almost all seen between Woolwich and Dartford, and in the six winters up to 1973/74 the peak counts have been two, eighteen, eight, five and thirty-two respectively. The latter count was on 2nd January, 1974 at Rainham, and in the same winter there were up to three in Limehouse Reach. It is interesting to note that the largest winter concentration of scaup in Britain occurs in the Firth of Forth, where up to 30,000 are seen annually. Like the Thames this is also a semi-polluted estuary, and it is perhaps surprising that more have not taken advantage of the improved situation which now exists, although traditionally scaup occur in large numbers in southern Britain only during very cold winters.

WILDFOWL—OCCASIONAL VISITORS

Black Swan

A pair, probably from one of the London park wildfowl collections, was present around Vauxhall Bridge during 1973, and another or one of the same birds frequented the Barking area during the summer of 1975.

Canada Goose

In view of the increasing abundance of this species in London, especially on the central park lakes, it is surprising that there is only one record for the Inner Thames, of two which frequented the Limehouse area in the early months of 1974.

Brent Goose

Skeins of geese are regularly seen flying over the London area, either as part of their normal movements in and out of Britain, or as a result of cold weather. The brent goose, however, is of very infrequent occurrence in the London area, so the series of records for the Inner Thames is of particular interest. The first were seen on the Swanscombe marshes in 1950, when there were up to fourteen during October and November. Since 1969 they have occurred annually, all within the period from 17th October to 22nd February. Of the ten separate sightings at least six refer to flocks heading west upriver. They almost certainly originate from the large population in the outer estuary, starting off on a direct overland route to the Channel. Apart from a flock of a hundred flying upriver past Tilbury on 8th November, 1975 (part of an exceptional overland movement described in Part Two) numbers have not exceeded fifteen. Only one observation refers to a bird settled on the foreshore of the river (at Rainham in October 1971), so clearly the area does not provide the right habitat and food to attract resident flocks as yet.

Ruddy Shelduck

A series of records of a female with the shelduck flocks in the Woolwich, Barking and Crossness sections from 18th February, 1973 until at least January 1975, probably all refer to the same individual. During the same period a female has also been seen intermittently on the North Kent Marshes, and the interchange of dates suggest that this was the same bird. Its presence in the Crossness area in June 1974 strongly suggests captive origin rather than a wild winter visitor. One seen at Swanscombe on 28th April, 1967 was later seen on the North Kent Marshes.

Mandarin

One with mallard at Barking on 16th November, 1974 was free-winged and shy, and probably originated from one of the local feral populations.

Gadwall

The main stronghold for this species in the London area is the Barn Elms reservoir in West London. Gadwall were first noted at this site during the 1930's, and the flock has gradually increased in size, a count of 130 in January 1973 being the highest ever. Not surprisingly, gadwall often join the mallard which flight from the reservoir to the adjacent parts of the Upper Thames, and counts there of between ten and forty are quite frequent.

Elsewhere on the Thames they are rather scarce. On the Inner Thames the first record was of one at Swanscombe in the autumn of 1959. Since 1973 they have become a little more frequent, but still the maximum seen on any one day is only four, and all records come from the sections between Blackwall Reach and Barking.

Garganey

Records of this summer visitor to Britain are confined to the suitable marsh areas along the Inner Thames: none has been seen on the river itself. By far the most observations come from Rainham Marsh, where it is more regular in autumn than in spring. Also at this site there has been a series of summer records since 1942, giving rise to suspicions of breeding on more than one occasion, but this has never been proved. Autumn passage takes place between

July and September. Numbers are usually small and the largest flock was sixteen at Rainham Marsh in August 1961.

Shoveler

Considering the large and annually increasing numbers of shoveler which frequent some of the London reservoirs, it is rather surprising that it has remained something of a rarity on the Inner Thames. Some of the riverside marshes, especially Rainham Marsh, can attract up to thirty in autumn and winter, but they are notably scarce on the river itself, but in the 1975/76 winter there were signs that the situation may be changing. Before then there had been only four records (maximum five birds) since 1960, but in the 1975/76 winter there was a small number present throughout in the Barking Bay, building up to a maximum of eleven in February.

It seems likely that recent changes in the invertebrate fauna of the river may have provided a suitable food to attract shoveler. This is an interesting development which will be closely watched.

26. A pair of shoveler.

Ferruginous Duck

In keeping with its status elsewhere in Britain, the ferruginous duck is an extremely rare visitor to the Inner Thames. None has been seen on the river itself, but there were two at riverside pits at Dartford early in 1951, and one at Swanscombe in March 1970. Since 1970/71 one or two have been seen each winter at Surrey Docks.

Long-tailed Duck

One at Rainham and Erith from 22nd to 29th October, 1972 is the only record for the Inner Thames.

Common Scoter

Since 1947 there have been ten records of scoter on the Inner Thames, and most of these refer to riverside pits rather than the river itself. All have been singles except two at Woolwich in November, 1970 and seven on 22nd July, 1971 at Dartford. Inland records of this exclusively marine duck usually involve storm-driven or sick birds, and this is probably the case with most of this series of records for the Inner Thames.

Goldeneye

Up to 1960 goldeneye had never been seen on the Inner Thames, but it has been recorded in seven of the sixteen years since then. The numbers involved have been small, the largest flock being five at Woolwich in January 1970. All have occurred downriver from Woolwich, except for one in Limehouse Reach in 1974/75.

Smew

Singles at Woolwich on 8th March and 6th December, 1969 and one at Dartford on 24th January, 1970. Goosander and smew are of fairly regular occurrence on the upper reaches of the Thames above London, and there is a regular wintering population on some of the London reservoirs, although this has been declining during the last decade. It is a possibility that the waters of the Inner Thames are not clear enough for fish-eating species like these and others to get at

27. A drake smew. A rare visitor to the river, though a regular one on London's reservoirs.

their prey, and this may account for their comparative rarity on the river.

Red-breasted Merganser

There are only four records for the Inner Thames: singles in March 1967 and November 1969, both at Dartford, two at Woolwich in November 1970, and one at Rainham in April 1974.

Goosander

There are only four records of goosander on the Inner Thames during the study period. Three are from Woolwich (singles apart from three on 12th January, 1969) and one at Purfleet on 1st January, 1972.

CHAPTER 4

WADERS AND OTHER SPECIES

✤

T HIS book is chiefly concerned with wildfowl, but in the case of the Inner Thames wading birds have formed an important part of the story. This chapter is therefore devoted to them and includes a short summary of other species which have been affected by the anti-pollution campaign.

Oystercatcher

In 1971 oystercatchers bred in the London area for the first time, on both the Swanscombe and Rainham Marshes. These breeding records were a remarkable climax to the general increase in the occurrence of oystercatchers in London in recent years, especially along the Thames and its marshes.

Until 1960 there had been only nine records involving mainly single birds, although five were seen at Dartford in January, 1954. After 1960 small numbers were recorded each year along the Thames, and for a few years before the nesting at Rainham and Swanscombe they became more frequent during the summer months. Although most sites on the Inner Thames upriver to Woolwich are visited from time to time, there has not been the general increase in numbers as with some other wader species, and parties in excess of four or five are very rare and those which have occurred are presumed migrant flocks, such as seven at Swanscombe in August 1960, twenty-two at Woolwich in December 1969 and fourteen at Swanscombe in August 1970: all three parties were seen flying west upriver.

Although oystercatchers have been seen regularly in the summer months along the Inner Thames, there has been only one further confirmed breeding record since 1971, at Rainham in 1973. Although the nest sites in all cases have been on riverside marsh areas, the adults have been seen feeding on the adjacent foreshore of

92

the river, and clearly the anti-pollution programme has been a major factor in providing London with a new nesting species.

Lapwing

The lapwing is a familiar bird of the marshes along the Inner Thames, both as a breeding bird and particularly in winter when flocks of over 1,000 occur regularly. Past data on lapwings along the river is scant, but what there is suggests that there has probably been little significant change in status, although it seems likely that habitat changes such as rubbish dumping, drainage and building would have reduced the breeding population.

Favoured areas for winter flocks are the Swanscombe Marshes, West Thurrock ash ponds and adjacent arable land, Dartford Marshes, Rainham/Aveley Marshes, and the tidal foreshore of the river itself which have all held concentrations of between 500 and 1,500 birds in recent years. Smaller gatherings occur at Barking and in the Thamesmead area. There is little indication of increasing use of the foreshore of the river as a result of the cleaner conditions: even during the height of the pollution between 1945 and 1950, John F. Burton found similar numbers on the marshes, and especially during hard weather large numbers resorted to the tidal foreshore. In recent years lapwing have been seen regularly along the river, but the westerly limit of regular flocks is the mouth of Barking Creek where there have been up to 200: further upstream their occurrence is rather erratic, and in very small numbers, and probably involves migrant birds resting temporarily.

Ringed Plover

The status of ringed plovers on the Inner Thames appears to have passed through several distinct phases during the present century, dependent upon the availability of suitable roosting and feeding areas, and the degree of pollution in the river.

At the beginning of the century Ticehurst recorded them as mainly winter visitors, and he remarked on their excursions right up to the wharves of South-east London. This wintering population soon disappeared, probably as a result of increasing pollution in the river, and in the period up to the late 1940's ringed plovers became very scarce on the Inner Thames.

Between 1945 and 1959 a series of observations suggested that ringed plovers were increasingly using the Thames foreshore during

93

the autumn migration, rarely further upriver than Erith. In the early part of the period numbers rarely exceeded twenty, but during the 1950's higher numbers became more frequent with a peak count of ninety-two at Stone in August 1954.

The availability of new habitat at Swanscombe between the late 1950's and 1963 led to a further change in status, when lagoons of Thames-dredged mud on the riverside marsh provided a high-tide roosting area which attracted flocks of up to 400 in autumn and 120 in winter. This area became overgrown and unsuitable in the early 1960's, and the flocks moved with the mud-dredging operations to new lagoons on the Rainham Marshes. From the autumn of 1963 to the present day the lagoons at Rainham have attracted ringed plover flocks of up to 285 in autumn and thirty-five in winter.

Despite these large concentrations at Swanscombe and Rainham, the numbers which used the Thames foreshore for feeding did not seem to increase much until the late 1960's. Around this time a new high-tide roost was established on the ash ponds of the West Thurrock power station, and since then this site has served as the focal point for birds which feed on the Thames foreshore in the reaches between Erith and Swanscombe. Highest counts usually occur during the autumn and a sizeable wintering population has now been established. Peak autumn and winter counts for recent years at the West Thurrock roost are shown in the table.

Table 9: *Peak autumn and winter ringed plover counts at West Thurrock, 1968 to 1976*

	68/69	69/70	70/71	71/72	72/73	73/74	74/75	75/76
Autumn	—	—	120	72	175	250	104	150
Winter	15	5	30	100	117	150	150	256

The wintering birds from the West Thurrock roost feed on the foreshore between Erith and Swanscombe. Smaller numbers use the Rainham section and these are probably from the Rainham Marsh lagoons. Further upriver ringed plovers are rarely seen on the foreshore of the Thames, and since 1960 more than fifteen have not been seen together.

The Inner Thames is by far the most important site in London for ringed plovers. Numbers elsewhere are very small and of irregular occurrence. It is clear that the establishment of a sizeable wintering population in recent years is largely due to the anti-pollution activity, which has rendered the foreshore of the river suitable as a feeding area.

Ringed plovers are very scarce breeders in the London area. A pair which nested near Dartford in 1957 was only the second to have done so in the London area this century. Since then they have bred almost annually along the Thames, mainly on the dried out mud of the lagoons at Swanscombe and Rainham, and of forty-eight pairs which had nested in London up to 1973, thirty-seven had used Thames-side sites.

Curlew

Apart from an exceptional wintering flock in the Purfleet area during the 1972/73 winter, curlew have occurred irregularly and in very small numbers on the tidal foreshore of the Inner Thames since the early 1960's. They have been seen as far upriver as the Woolwich bay, in parties never exceeding four. On the marshes bordering the river there was a series of records of comparatively

28. So far curlew have not established a regular presence on the Inner Thames.

large flocks during the arctic conditions of 1962/63, with up to thirty-eight at Rainham, and forty-five at Dartford.

If anything there has been a slight decline in status since 1945 to 1950, during which period John F. Burton described curlew as occurring frequently in autumn and winter, with parties of up to nine upriver as far as Crossness.

Throughout the 1972/73 winter a flock of up to forty-three frequented the Purfleet and Swanscombe sections, flighting to roost at high tide on the ash ponds of West Thurrock power station and the adjacent arable land. Hopes that the species might subsequently have become established as a winter resident on the Inner Thames did not materialise, and since then its status as a scarce visitor has returned. There is no obvious reason why the influx should have been of such a temporary nature, but it is interesting that since the same winter the population of ruff in the Purfleet area has also declined. It is thought that the main food taken by both species was *Nereid* worms, and it may be that local changes in the availability of this food have occurred.

Redshank

Past records suggest that redshank were able to tolerate the polluted conditions of the Inner Thames better than other species of waders. Even between 1945 and 1950 when the state of the river was so deplorable, John F. Burton found that flocks of around a hundred were frequent on the foreshore below Erith, but they were extremely rare further upriver. It was at that time by far the commonest wader on the Inner Thames, and although nowadays it is greatly exceeded by dunlin in total numbers, it has shown an equally significant increase and upriver spread with the cleaner conditions.

The first signs that the situation was changing came during the cold spells at the beginning of the 1960's, when unprecedented numbers occurred on the lower reaches. In the particularly cold weather of 1962/63, for example, there were up to 300 redshank at Rainham and 250 at Dartford. At the time this was largely attributed to the arctic weather conditions, but in retrospect the anti-pollution programme which was beginning to take effect at that time seems likely to have been an additional factor.

The main colonisation of the Inner Thames did not get under way until the mid-1960's, however, and the subsequent counts are summarised in the table. The main concentrations are in the

swans by Beckton outfall.

xed raft of duck at high tide.

Tubifex worms in shallow water.

Green seaweeds covering the rocks at the western end of Woolwich Bay.

Tubifex 'fishermen' at work.

Life returns to the river: Ragworm in Woolwich Bay.

Table 10: Peak winter counts of redshank at Inner Thames sites, 1965/66 to 1975/76

	Upper and Lower Pool	Limehouse Reach	Greenwich Reach	Blackwall Reach	Bugsby's Reach	Woolwich Reach	Woolwich Arsenal	Woolwich	Barking	Crossness	Rainham	Erith	Dartford	Purfleet	Swanscombe	Thurrock	MINIMUM TOTAL
1965/66	—	—	—	—	—	—	—	—	—	—	—	—	—	—	—	—	—
1966/67	—	—	—	—	—	—	—	—	—	—	—	—	150	50	50	—	150
1967/68	—	—	—	—	—	—	—	—	—	—	—	—	50	—	—	—	50
1968/69	—	—	—	—	—	—	—	—	—	—	100	—	150	—	80	—	150
1969/70	—	—	—	—	—	—	—	—	—	—	110	—	200	—	420	—	420
1970/71	—	—	—	—	—	—	—	33	1	4	130	25	600	320	300	463	958
1971/72	—	—	—	—	—	—	—	23	14	15	124	62	200	200	170	100	434
1972/73	—	—	—	—	—	—	—	—	—	13	40	17	200	700	120	124	799
1973/74	......c50 total*							2	6	—	—	10	250	460	120	—	520
1974/75	......c20 total*							10	12	—	120	—	—	530	180	—	627
1975/76	—	—	—	1	2	—	—	—	3	2	81	—	—	380	—	—	381

* Mainly roosting birds at Surrey Commercial Docks

Rainham to Thurrock sections of the river, although since 1971/72 there has been a significant upriver shift of small numbers.

The ash ponds of the West Thurrock power station have become of major importance to the Inner Thames redshank population. The vast majority of the birds which feed on the river fly in to this site at high tide, which provides an extensive and secluded roost. Smaller numbers use other sites at high tide, at Swanscombe saltings, Dartford Marshes, Aveley saltings, Rainham Marsh and Crossness. Since 1973 up to forty-nine birds have used the disused Surrey Docks as a high tide roost, and this is probably the focal point for the population which feeds on the upriver sections above Woolwich.

Redshank have bred for years in good numbers on the marshes which border the river. In the 1950's the population was estimated at around eighty pairs and now around thirty pairs nest annually. Much of this reduction is the result of local habitat changes, such as drainage, large-scale refuse tipping, ploughing and building.

Snipe

As far as the tidal foreshore of the Inner Thames is concerned, snipe greatly favour those sections which are bordered by saltings: peak counts at such sites during the study period since 1968/69 have been 150 in 1972/73 at Swanscombe, 300 at Aveley saltings in 1971/72 and fifty at Crayford Ness saltings in 1972/73. Such high counts are usually the result of cold weather conditions, and the 'normal' winter population of the foreshore of the whole London to Tilbury section is much less at around ninety. On the riverside marshes the population can be quite large, much depending on the severity of the weather and the dampness of the habitat from winter to winter: in recent winters there have been up to 400 at Dartford Marshes, 300 at Swanscombe Marshes and a hundred in the Thamesmead area. The upriver limits of snipe are the Woolwich and Barking bays and the mouth of Barking Creek, although numbers at these sites rarely exceed ten.

As a breeding bird on the Inner Thames marshes, numbers have declined drastically during this century, and during the last decade there is only a handful of possible or proved nesting records.

Jack Snipe

The jack snipe is of regular occurrence in small numbers on the marshes along the Inner Thames. Some exceptionally high counts have been made in recent winters, for example up to twenty at Dartford Marshes in 1968/69, twenty to twenty-five at Swanscombe in 1969/70 and up to fifteen at Rainham Marsh in 1970/71.

Knot

The knot is an extremely erratic visitor to the Inner Thames, and there is little evidence to suggest that its status has changed much in recent years as a result of the cleaner conditions. Elsewhere in the Thames Estuary and in southern Britain its numbers vary according to the severity of the winter, and this is reflected to some extent in the counts for the Inner Thames. Up to the 1950's there were no records of more than ten together, and all counts since then are summarised in the table (all occurred in the Rainham to Swanscombe sections).

Table 11: *Peak counts of knot on the Inner Thames, 1952/53 to 1974/75. All occurred in the Rainham to Swanscombe sections.*

1952/53	1953/54	1955/56	1960/61	1961/62	1962/63	1963/64
10	10	20	250*	51*	15*	3

1965/66	1968/69	1969/70	1970/71	1971/72	1972/73	1973/74	1974/75
1	30	250	40	1	3	10	1

* Counts from Swanscombe dredged mud lagoons rather than the foreshore of the river.

Dunlin

Writing in 1921, P. W. Horn noted that he had seen dunlin at a date not specified 'so numerous over the flat towards Purfleet as to give the impression of a drifting smoke cloud.' This is one of the few pieces of evidence which shows the abundance of some species on the Inner Thames before the great wave of pollution during the present century took its toll of wildlife on the river.

There is plenty of evidence of the resultant dearth of birds, however. In the case of dunlin, for example, John F. Burton rarely saw parties of more than twenty between 1945 and 1950 during his studies of the Thames and its marshes. This situation did not alter much until the late 1950's, when quite unprecedented numbers of

29. Dunlin seen against the background of West Thurrock Power Station.

dunlin for the London area began roosting on the newly-created dredged-mud lagoons on Swanscombe Marsh. In the winter of 1960/61 a peak of 2,500 was using this roost, flighting to downriver sites beyond Cliffe to feed. At some time during the mid-1960's increasing numbers began to use the tidal foreshore of the Inner Thames as a feeding area. Since then there has been a remarkable increase in numbers during the winter months, combined with a gradual upriver spread, both trends clearly associated with the improving cleanliness of the river, as shown by Table 12.

With the end of mud-dredging operations at Swanscombe, the roost site there had become unsuitable in the early 1960's, and the Inner Thames feeding population has moved to new roost sites. By far the most important of these are the ash ponds of the West Thurrock power station, which is used by all the birds which feed in the Erith to Swanscombe sections, and numbers there have exceeded

Table 12: Peak winter counts of dunlin at Inner Thames sites, 1967/68 to 1975/76. Only counts of birds using the Inner Thames as a feeding area are included

	Upper and Lower Pool	Limehouse Reach	Greenwich Reach	Blackwall Reach	Bugsby's Reach	Woolwich Reach	Woolwich Arsenal	Woolwich	Barking	Crossness	Rainham	Erith	Dartford	Purfleet	Swanscombe	Thurrock	MINIMUM TOTAL
1967/68	—	—	—	—	—	—	—	—	—	—	—	—	—	—	800	—	800
1968/69	—	—	—	—	—	—	—	—	—	—	—	—	1500	—	1500	—	1800
1969/70	—	—	—	—	—	—	—	1000	—	—	—	—	4000	—	1500	—	4000
1970/71	—	—	—	—	—	—	—	1100	—	1100	750	300	5000	2800	3500	500	6000
1971/72	—	—	—	—	—	—	—	1800	30	3000	1500	20	1500	3000	1750	100	5800
1972/73	—	—	—	—	—	—	—	2000	203	2000	1390	200	6000	6000	1200	640	7455
1973/74	—	550	—	400	150	1650	—	1000	750	1300	600	400	4000	7000	600	—	7000
1974/75	—	450	—	550	900	900	—	380	1500	150	800	—	700	5000	700	—	4800
1975/76	—	—	—	—	5	600	600	100	210	250	1450	—	10	5000	—	—	5000

7,000 in recent winters. Other important roosts are on the dredged mud lagoons on Rainham Marsh (up to 1,800), Aveley saltings (up to 1,000), Crossness sewage works sludge ponds (up to 1,000), Dartford Marshes and Swanscombe Marshes. In 1974/75 up to 400 used pools behind the new river wall at Thamesmead.

Observations show that there is an upriver movement ahead of the incoming tide to take full advantage of the exposed mud for feeding. Thus the reaches above Woolwich are occupied by feeding birds towards the end of the tide cycle, and the birds involved return back downriver, possibly the whole length of the Inner Thames as far as the West Thurrock roost. A few of these upriver feeding birds have been sighted flying north up the Lea valley, but no permanent roost site has yet been discovered there. In recent winters very small numbers have used the disused Surrey Commercial Docks at high tide, and it is perhaps surprising that the large numbers which feed in the adjacent reaches do not make more use of this area as a roost.

Ruff

Up to the 1950's ruff were unknown on the Inner Thames and its marshes. Between 1952 and 1967/68 there was a marked change in status, and during this period they were seen almost annually in small numbers. This corresponded with a general increase in records in the London area as a whole, and on the Inner Thames this trend was clearly helped by the availability of new, highly suitable habitat in the form of dredged mud lagoons on the Swanscombe and Rainham Marshes. During this period the records were almost entirely confined to riverside marsh areas rather than the foreshore, and the larger counts occurred in autumn. All records are summarised in the table.

Table 13: *Peak counts of ruff on the Inner Thames, 1952/53 to 1967/68.*
Records during this period were almost entirely confined to riverside marsh areas rather than the foreshore itself. An asterisk denotes autumn rather than winter count.

	1952/ 1953	1953/ 1954	1954/ 1955	1955/ 1956	1956/ 1957	1957/ 1958	1958/ 1959	1959/ 1960
Purfleet/ Swanscombe	—	—	—	—	7	6	8*	9*
Dartford	1*	14*	3*	5	—	5	4	—
Rainham	—	—	—	—	—	—	—	10*

	1960/ 1961	1961/ 1962	1962/ 1963	1963/ 1964	1964/ 1965	1965/ 1966	1966/ 1967	1967/ 1968
Purfleet/ Swanscombe	23*	8	5	—	1	—	—	—
Dartford	3	—	8	3	1	—	—	1
Rainham	—	—	32*	—	22*	—	15*	14*

Since 1967/68 there has been a major change in the status of ruff. A sizeable wintering population has been established, which feeds on the tidal foreshore in the Dartford, Purfleet and Swanscombe sections, and roosts at high tide on the ash ponds of the West Thurrock power station, but numbers have declined in more recent winters. This colonisation has clearly been due to the improved cleanliness of the river, which has also benefitted several other species of wader. Peak counts of this population are summarised in the following table.

Table 14: *Peak winter counts of ruff on the Dartford to Swanscombe sections of the Inner Thames, 1968/69 to 1974/75*

1968/69	1969/70	1970/71	1971/72	1972/73	1973/74	1974/75
75	120	130	68	100	48	24

The reason for the decline in recent winters is not fully understood, but the main food taken by ruff on the Inner Thames is thought to be *Nereid* worms, and perhaps there has been a change in the availability of this food. When at its peak this population was the largest winter concentration in Britain, and the numbers involved were remarkable for a species whose usual winter range is in Africa.

Since 1967/68 sizeable numbers have continued to visit the Rainham Marshes dredged mud lagoons, with up to sixty in autumn and forty-eight in winter, and there may have been some interchange between this site and the ash ponds at West Thurrock. The similar site on Swanscombe Marshes became disused and unsuitable in the early 1960's. Ruff are scarce on the river above Rainham, and there are only four records for the foreshore itself, the most together being three at Woolwich in September, 1970. Three were seen at the disused Surrey Commercial Docks on 7th February, 1975.

Grey Plover

Since 1950 one or two grey plover have occurred almost annually on the Inner Thames. In the severe 1962/63 winter up to five were present for most of the time, and since 1970/71 one or two have been resident in the Rainham to Swanscombe area throughout the winter. Grey plover have now been seen on the Inner Thames in all months of the year except June. The largest count is six at Dartford on 28th December, 1969.

Golden Plover

There are no sites on the marshes of the Inner Thames which attract a resident winter flock of golden plover. Those records which do exist refer in the main to migrant flocks flying over, otherwise numbers rarely exceed ten.

Little Ringed Plover

Although it occurs regularly in spring and autumn at riverside sites along the Inner Thames, it is rarely if ever seen on the tidal foreshore. In recent years by far the largest concentrations have been seen on Rainham Marsh, where the dredged mud lagoons have attracted over fifty on occasions in autumn. A few pairs nest annually at suitable sites such as Swanscombe, Dartford Marshes, Rainham Marshes and in the Thamesmead area. In 1973 a pair bred successfully at the disused Surrey Commercial Docks, the first record of proved breeding in Inner London.

Kentish Plover

Singles at Rainham Marsh on 1st July, 1962 and 18th April, 1970 and Swanscombe Marsh on 6th May, 1972 are the only records.

Avocet

A scarce visitor to the foreshore and marshes of the Inner Thames. In 1952/53 one frequented the ash ponds of Littlebrook power station and adjacent parts of the river from 22nd December to 24th

January. Six further records are: one at West Thurrock 4th April, 1956, one at Littlebrook 6th April, 1958, one at Rainham 21st April, 1968, three at Rainham 23rd March, 1969, one at Rainham 4th July, 1970, and two at Rainham 15th October, 1973.

30. A little ringed plover's nest amid the rubble of demolished warehouses at Surrey Docks.

Whimbrel

Very small numbers are seen occasionally on the Inner Thames marshes in spring and autumn. The only record of whimbrel feeding on the Thames foreshore was in August, 1948 when one was seen at the mouth of Dartford Creek by John F. Burton.

Black-tailed Godwit

Chiefly a scarce early autumn visitor to riverside marsh sites along the Inner Thames. In recent years most have occurred on the dredged mud lagoons on Rainham Marsh, the peak count there being sixteen during July, 1970. A new departure in the spring of both 1974 and 1975 was the occupation of possible breeding sites at two different areas, but as yet there has been no proof of attempted nesting.

Bar-tailed Godwit

There has been a total of only twenty-three records of bar-tailed godwit on the Inner Thames since 1947. A breakdown of these shows that the great majority occur during April and May: none of these stay for long and the movement is clearly an offshoot of the major passage involving many thousands through the English Channel which occurs at this time. An interesting confirmation of this involves a flock of thirteen birds which was seen flying east over Staines Reservoir in west London on 28th April, 1974 and later seen at Rainham. This is also the largest flock recorded on the Inner Thames.

Table 15: *Breakdown of all records of bar-tailed godwit on the Inner Thames, 1947 to 1974/75*

Jan	Feb	Mar	Apr	May	Jun	Jul	Aug	Sep	Oct	Nov	Dec	
1	1	—	8	5	—	2	2	3	—	—	1	Number of records
1	1	—	40	16	—	4	4	4	—	—	2	number of birds

Spotted Redshank

A regular autumn migrant in small numbers on the riverside marshes. At Rainham Marsh the largest gathering in recent years was eleven in late August 1969. In spring it is much scarcer, and a flock of six seen by John Swift at Aveley saltings on 17th June, 1973 was exceptional, and was one of the few occasions that this species has been seen on the foreshore of the river. Spotted redshanks are occasionally seen in winter, and in 1973/74 one was present throughout, associating with the redshank flocks in the Rainham to Purfleet section.

31. Spotted redshank.

Marsh Sandpiper

One was seen at Rainham Marsh from 26th to 28th August, 1963 and at Swanscombe Marsh from 26th August to 3rd September. Almost certainly it was the same bird commuting between the two sites. It was about the fifteenth of this South-east European wader to have been seen in Britain.

Greenshank

A few visit the wader areas along the Inner Thames during the spring and autumn migrations. More than four together at any one time is exceptional.

Green Sandpiper

A regular and sometimes numerous visitor to the Inner Thames marshes during the autumn migration. In recent years it has been most numerous on the dredged mud lagoons on Rainham Marsh, where around fifteen are regular between mid-July and mid-September and up to fifty were there in August, 1970. A few are seen throughout the winter and spring along the Inner Thames, and the river saltings are visited occasionally.

Solitary Sandpiper

One was located at Rainham Marsh on 1st September, 1974. It stayed in the area until the 6th, and constituted the fourteenth record for Britain of this North American species.

Wood Sandpiper

Much scarcer than the green sandpiper, and records are entirely restricted to the autumn migration period. Up to ten have been seen in recent years on Rainham Marsh, which is the present stronghold of the species on the Inner Thames.

Common Sandpiper

More widespread and common on the Inner Thames than the green and wood sandpiper. It is less specialised in its choice of habitat, and a few are seen each autumn in the upper reaches towards London, and it more frequently visits the tidal foreshore. At Rainham Marsh in recent years thirty or forty has been the regular autumn peak count, the main migration occurring between July and September. It has been estimated that the total population of the Inner Thames and its marshes at peak times during the autumn migration must regularly exceed 150 birds. Many fewer occur in spring and summer, and around ten probably winter regularly along the Inner Thames.

Turnstone

A few turnstone have occurred annually along the Inner Thames since 1950: most are seen on the riverside feeding/roosting areas rather than the foreshore itself. Numbers are generally very small, and eleven at Rainham Marsh on 24th August, 1968 is the largest flock. A monthly breakdown of fifty-one dated occurrences since 1950 indicates that the majority of birds involved are on passage, with a main peak between July and September, and a smaller one in spring in May.

Table 16: *Breakdown of fifty-one dated records of turnstone on the Inner Thames, 1950 to 1974/75*

Jan	Feb	Mar	Apr	May	Jun	Jul	Aug	Sep	Oct	Nov	Dec	
2	3	1	3	7	—	9	14	7	2	1	2	number of records
3	5	1	5	17	—	15	52	14	3	3	5	number of birds

Sanderling

A scarce visitor to the Inner Thames, which has been reported in thirteen of the twenty-one years since 1954. Dated occurrences are summarised in the table which shows a marked spring and autumn migration peak in May and September. Most of the winter records are associated with cold weather.

Table 17: *Breakdown of thirty-four dated records of sanderling on the Inner Thames, 1954 to 1974*

Jan	Feb	Mar	Apr	May	Jun	Jul	Aug	Sep	Oct	Nov	Dec	
2	5	—	—	10	—	2	5	7	1	1	1	number of records
2	25	—	—	16	—	3	8	21	1	1	1	number of birds

The largest flocks are sixteen, feeding at the mouth of the River Darent, during severe weather on 1st February, 1956 and ten at Rainham on 20th September, 1967.

Semi-palmated Sandpiper

One was seen at pools behind the river wall at Barking on 4th May, 1974. It was the first time that this extremely rare vagrant from North America had been seen in spring in Britain.

Western Sandpiper

One was located and identified on the dredged mud lagoons at Rainham Marsh in July 1973. It was present from 21st to 23rd, and associated with little stints and dunlin. This constituted only the second record for Britain of this Nearctic species.

Little Stint

Although predominantly an autumn visitor to the marshes along the Inner Thames, it has been recorded in all months of the year. Numbers seen during the autumn passage, which takes place from late July to late September, vary according to the strength of the migration elsewhere in Britain. Over thirty have been seen in good autumns on Rainham Marsh, and a few sometimes winter there, and six or seven did so in 1968/69. A few are occasionally seen on the foreshore of the river, when they associate with the dunlin flocks.

Temminck's Stint

This rarity is occasionally seen on the marshes along the Inner Thames, and in recent years it has been seen almost annually on Rainham Marsh. Exceptionally, three were present there at the end of August 1970, and one wintered in 1970/71, sometimes joining the dunlin on the foreshore at Aveley saltings.

Pectoral Sandpiper

One at Rainham Marsh from 30th September to 3rd October, 1971, is the only record along the Inner Thames for this rare North American wader.

Purple Sandpiper

This marine coast wader which normally inhabits rocky shores in winter is extremely scarce on the Inner Thames. One was trapped and ringed at Dartford on 3rd January, 1970 and stayed for the most of the month. Singles on 24th January, 1971 and 21st December, 1973 were also seen at Dartford. All three were feeding on the foreshore and adjacent saltings.

Curlew Sandpiper

A fairly regular autumn migrant to wader sites along the Inner Thames. Numbers vary greatly according to the strength of curlew sandpiper migration elsewhere in Britain from autumn to autumn. In spring there are only occasional records. At Rainham Marsh

110

32. An immature curlew sandpiper, a fairly regular visitor to the Inner Thames.

which in recent years has offered the best marsh-wader habitat along the river, the largest count was seventy in late August and early September 1969. In good years a few may resort to the tidal foreshore.

OTHER SPECIES

As well as wildfowl and waders, several other species have benefitted greatly from the increasing cleanliness of the Inner Thames, and they form just as important a part of the story.

The fish life which has returned as a result of the anti-pollution programme has attracted several fish-eating species. For years the Inner Thames has been known as a migratory flyway for terns moving west in autumn, but since the mid-1960's feeding flocks have been noted with increasing regularity and this is an entirely new phenomenon. Largest concentrations are in late July to

111

September, especially around the power stations at Dartford and West Thurrock. The last site is particularly productive and the main food which attracts the terns is apparently the proliferation of brown shrimps which pass into the river from the fish screens of the cooling water intake. Common terns are invariably the most numerous species, and since 1972 peak numbers have topped a hundred each autumn, the largest counts being 500 in 1966 and 350 in 1973. One or two Arctic terns have been identified among the flock in recent years, as have up to forty black terns and a few little terns and Sandwich terns. Occasional Arctic skuas are seen on the Inner Thames, obviously attracted by the terns, and in 1972 one was present from 2nd to 30th September spending much of the time harrying common terns around the West Thurrock outfall.

Considering the abundance of fish now inhabiting the Inner Thames it is perhaps surprising that some fish-eating species have not become more numerous than is in fact the case. Cormorants are regularly seen below Rainham, and occasionally as far upriver as Greenwich, but the total population of the Inner Thames has apparently never exceeded ten. Red-throated divers and, rarely, black-throated divers have occurred from time to time, but there has been no marked increase in recent years and there is nothing to suggest that the occurrences continue to involve other than oiled or storm-driven birds. Great crested grebes are scarce on the Inner Thames, and more than two have never been seen together. Exceptionally, there was a red-necked grebe on the river at Rainham on 27th July, 1951 and six slavonian grebes were reported offshore at Barking on 2nd April, 1974. The scarcity of fish-eating wildfowl like goosander, red-breasted merganser and smew has already been commented on. It has been suggested that poor underwater visibility prevents these species from catching their prey easily. It is unlikely that this situation will change much in the future, for the Thames is inherently a heavily silted river, and much of it is unavoidably carried in suspension in the water.

A few coot and moorhens join with the wildfowl flocks in some parts of the river, attracted by the green algae *Enteromorpha sp.* which grows on the river walls and pilings and provides their main food. Both species were unknown on the river only a few years ago, and their presence is due to the clean-up which has led to a prolific growth of this plant, which can live only in oxygenated water. The main sites for coot, together with peak counts, are: Upper Pool, twelve; Woolwich, thirty-five; Crossness, forty-three. The peak total count for the Inner Thames during the study period since 1968 was

:cting worm samples from the Inner Thames mud. The two authors are on the left.

elduck 'tubifexing'.

fifty-six during the 1972/73 winter. The moorhen is much scarcer, and the total for the whole Inner Thames below London Bridge has never exceeded ten, although there was a party of up to twelve further upstream around Southwark and Blackfriars Bridges in 1971.

Herons feed in small numbers on the foreshore of the Inner Thames, but most frequent the riverside marshes. A roost for up to fifteen has recently been established on the jetty of the disused Beckton gas works in the Barking section. At Surrey Docks up to fifty used to gather in the early 1970's, but recently numbers have been much lower. The vast majority of herons seen along the Inner Thames probably come from the large heronry at the Walthamstow reservoirs, and the small one in Regent's Park: highest numbers occur in late summer when juveniles from these sites arrive. On the lower reaches of the Inner Thames a higher proportion of herons may originate from the Northward Hill heronry on the North Kent Marshes.

Gulls are so numerous on the Inner Thames, especially during the

33 & 34. Certainly the most unexpected visitor to the Inner Thames, this glossy ibis was photographed at Swanscombe.

winter, that very often they defy counting. In addition vast flocks gather on London's main refuse tips at Barking, Rainham and Stone. The enormous increase in wintering gulls inland since the beginning of this century is well known, and in the London area this was undoubtedly helped by the sewer-like conditions on the Thames in which gulls thrived. Few censuses have been carried out in recent years, but estimates during the BTO/RSPB Birds of Estuaries Enquiry show that the Inner Thames holds up to 1,600 Scandinavian lesser black-backed gulls, which is the largest concentration in the country. Numbers of great black-backed gulls and herring gulls were estimated as comparable with those of lesser black-backed gulls, but numbers of black-headed gulls and common gulls are obviously very much greater and total in excess of 50,000. With so many gulls around it is not surprising that rare species have been identified among the flocks: glaucous gull, Mediterranean gull, little gull and kittiwake have been seen on several occasions in recent years.

Although of not much scientific interest, there is no doubt that the unusual or rare species which we have encountered on our studies of the Inner Thames have added to our enjoyment. Perhaps the most unexpected were a glossy ibis which spent a month on the foreshore at Swanscombe in the spring of 1973, busily pulling *Nereid* worms from the mud, and a sub-adult gannet which flew past our astonished eyes at the Woolwich Ferry a few weeks later, heading towards the heart of London. Our companion on the latter occasion was Dr Eugene Novak, who was able to 'tick off' a new life species, at a place as unlikely for gannets as his native Poland!

35. The authors counting from the shore at Barking Bay.

PART II
THE NORTH KENT MARSHES
AND THE
SOUTH ESSEX SHORE

CHAPTER 5

AN AREA OF INTERNATIONAL IMPORTANCE

⚜

THE North Kent Marshes extend from Gravesend in the west to Shellness at the end of the Swale channel in the east, a distance of twenty-five miles. These superb marshes, forming a famous entity in themselves on the southern shore of the Thames Estuary, can be divided into three distinct areas.

The central one is the Medway Estuary from Lower Upnor, just east of Chatham to its narrow mouth at Sheerness. The brackish-freshwater grazing marshes of the Chetney peninsula which separate the Medway from the Swale form an integral part of the Medway so far as wildfowl are concerned, large scale flight lines crossing the western wall in contrast to the eastern one.

The Medway Estuary behind its narrow mouth opens out into a huge tidal basin, characterised by large and small saltmarsh islands and a maze of creeks, largely formed in the second half of the eighteenth century when the Roman walls embanking the main channel gave way. The Romans must have managed the estuary with masterly skill for the walls to have lasted so long and their famous Upchurch pottery can be found in many parts of the south shore to this day. However, in 1376 a Writ was issued by King Edward III ordering the Bishop of Rochester to repair the seawalls. Although the islands were much more extensive when first formed, the rate of erosion has lessened, but the advent of the Thames Barrage may change this for the worse.

The second area, the Swale channel, separates the Isle of Sheppey from the Kentish mainland and extends from Queenborough in the west to Shellness in the east. The westerly third is narrow and here the island is linked to the mainland by the road and rail bridge at Kingsferry, the newest bridge being built after the great surge tide of 31st January, 1953.

The eastern two-thirds of the Swale are wider, with extensive mud and sandbanks and small areas of salting, while the southern third of the island is composed of extensive grazing marshes, traditionally used for sheep, but quite large areas are now being turned over to cereals.

Thirdly, there is the Kentish shore of the Thames Estuary which extends from Higham Bay to the Isle of Grain, with its extensive intertidal mudflat known as Blythe Sand and Roas Bank. It is fortunate for Kent that the deep water channel of the Thames along Sea Reach keeps close to the Essex shore, so that these marshes have so far been spared such developments as Tilbury docks and the great oil refinery complexes at Thames Haven and Canvey Island.

There is little saltmarsh along the Kentish Thames, but there is a magnificent stretch of brackish and freshwater grazing marshes along the whole of the northern side of the Cliffe peninsula, overlooked by the wooded slopes of Northward Hill, site of Europe's largest heronry. As on Sheppey, some of these traditional grazing marshes are being converted to cereals.

Ecologically, each area supports three main zones: the intertidal zone, the saltmarshes and, inland of the sea wall, brackish marshes and their water systems, in which the water gradually becomes fresher the further it lies inland.

Many of these water systems can be seen to follow the line of former tidal creeks, the result of land reclamation, which reached a peak in the mid-nineteenth century. Strangely enough, this was not brought about by the need for more agricultural land, but was in fact spurred on by two major cholera epidemics which swept across the whole of the area. Two rows of children's tombstones, thirteen in all, lie side by side in Cooling churchyard, clustered around an adult headstone in what is known traditionally as 'Pip's Church' from its association with Charles Dickens's *Great Expectations*. It is still possible to read two of the dates on the stones – 1771 and 1774 – and it seems likely that these little children were indeed victims of cholera, although malaria was also said to have been rife.

Be that as it may, even before this, the North Kent Marshes obviously had a dreadful reputation for ill health and were considered by the Admiralty as ideal for isolating plague and yellow fever contacts at the end of the seventeenth century. These pathetic people were kept on board ships anchored off Deadman's Island, just north of Chetney. Deadman's Island must have been given its name at that time, being of course the place where these victims were taken ashore and buried. To this day one has only to wade across Shepherd's Creek to Deadman's to be able to find human bones with no effort, a surprising number showing signs of osteomyelitis – a chronic bone infection – which must have been very prevalent in those days.

In March 1752, Chetney Hill was selected by the Admiralty as the site for the first shore-based Lazaret – a plague quarantine unit – but work was finally abandoned in 1812, the footings being unsound, so that walls cracked and roofs fell in. Sir William Pym in his report to Parliament described the area as 'the most unhealthy spot in England'.

It may seem strange now to realise that it was the eradication of disease which led to the development of the North Kent Marshes as we know them today. In this respect of course there is a similarity with the Inner Thames.

The intertidal zone is extensive throughout the whole area, characterised almost entirely by mudflats rather than sandbanks, except in the eastern Swale. These are highly productive biologically, nurturing seaweeds, both green and brown, invertebrate marine animals, especially molluscs and crustacea, and

36. Marsh samphire flats on the Chetney peninsula.

fish. These in turn support a massive population of wildfowl, waders and other waterfowl at the upper end of the food chain.

The vegetation of the saltmarshes is typical of South-East England, varying according to their height and therefore the time that the plants are covered by the tide. The lower levels tend to be colonised by cordgrass (*Spartina*), used as resting cover by wildfowl, marsh samphire and glasswort, the lowest levels supporting both green and brown seaweeds and eel-grasses of two species *Zostera nana* and *Z. angustifolia*, which have shown a welcome tendency to recolonise the area during the past fifteen years, having been destroyed by disease in the 1930's.

The middle levels between high and low water are colonised by sea purslane, seablite and sea lavender and the highest levels by sea aster, hastate orache, the beautiful local species golden samphire and the saltmarsh grasses, red fescue and sea meadow grass.

THE MEDWAY ESTUARY

Dealing in turn with each of the three areas, it is appropriate to start with the Medway Estuary, for it forms the very heart of the North Kent Marshes and is, furthermore, of immense international importance for its wintering population of waterfowl.

The International Waterfowl Research Bureau has collected a vast amount of numerical data since 1967 in order to assess the international importance of all wetlands throughout the Palearctic. The winter population of the North-West European Region, which includes the British Isles, is the best known region at present, so that these international evaluations are of the utmost significance. This work was summarised in a brilliant paper by George Atkinson-Willes at the International Conference on the Conservation of Wetlands and Waterfowl held at Heiligenhafen, West Germany, in December 1974.

It was agreed at Heiligenhafen that any Wetland which held one per cent or more of the regional population of any species in mid-winter or held a combined total of over 10,000 individuals was of international importance. On this basis, the Medway was the only estuary in the United Kingdom regularly to hold over one per cent of four duck species, namely teal, wigeon, pintail and shelduck, as well as the Russian brent goose, and on occasions shoveler. In addition, in every mid-January International Census, it has held in excess of 10,000 head since 1969, even in the exceptionally mild winter of 1974–75.

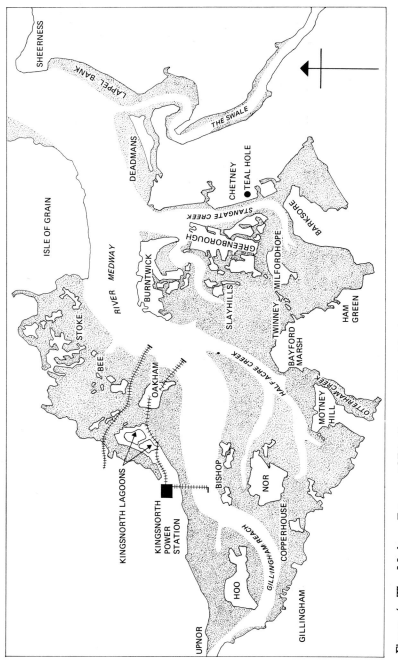

Figure 4. The Medway Estuary 1976. Compare this with the map on page 133, showing the land reclaimed by the Romans and lost since the eighteenth century.

The quite remarkable increases which have occurred can best be appreciated in tabulated form.

Table 18: *Peak counts of the predominant species on the Medway Estuary 1952–1976 with the international one per cent qualifying figure in brackets for each species.*

Years	1952–61	1962–65	1966–68	1969–71
Mallard (10,000)	280	1200	2250	2500
Teal (1500)	2100	2180	1700	4500
Wigeon (4000)	1650	3100	5300	8500
Pintail (500)	95	300	320	910
Shoveler (200)	150	84	265	420
Shelduck (1250)	1100	1500	3000	3000
Russian Brent (700)	105	110	230	450

Seasons*	1971–72	1972–73	1973–74	1974–75	1975–76
Mallard (10,000)	2450	1300	1630	3600	3450
Teal (1500)	4300	5100	5565	3495	6700
Wigeon (4000)	8200	8400	9456	4610	8700
Pintail (500)	1250	958	935	802	1400
Shoveler (200)	305	230	149	268	400
Shelduck (1250)	3270	2850	2450	2290	3250
Russian Brent (700)	550	750	766	716	1140

* September to February inclusive.

Table 19: *Mid-January wildfowl totals 1969–1976.*

1969:	10,446	1973:	17,006
1970:	15,207	1974:	18,319
1971:	15,308	1975:	12,202
1972:	16,136	1976:	21,510

We are also able to assess the Medway in considerable detail as a result of the work of Tony Prater, National Organiser of the Birds of Estuaries Enquiry since 1969. It is now known that the Medway is the most important UK estuary for teal and is in the top five UK estuaries for shelduck, pintail, wigeon and shoveler.

As a nesting area for wildfowl, the Medway was last surveyed in 1972, when 381 pairs were found, made up of 206 pairs of mallard, 129 pairs of shelduck, sixteen pairs of shoveler, twelve pairs of pochard and with smaller numbers of teal, wigeon, pintail, garganey,

37. An icy scene on the Medway in 1963.

tufted duck, greylag and mute swan. Although waders are not being detailed in this section, there were in addition 525 pairs of waders, giving a combined total of 906 pairs of waterfowl of eighteen species. Tony Prater's data showed that the Medway on those figures was supporting the fifth largest breeding population of these two bird groups in England. The only areas with more were the enormous complexes of the Solway, the Wash, Morecambe Bay and the Ribble Estuary; but the Medway had a diversity of species which could not be matched elsewhere.

As if this was not enough, the Medway now holds in winter almost 20,000 wading birds, including up to eight per cent of the wintering UK population of grey plovers and one per cent of dunlin and redshank and some of the largest flocks of spotted redshank. Indeed the grey plover represents over one per cent of the entire North-West European population.

Little wonder then, that conservationists have been extremely worried in recent years as threat after threat has been revealed, each of which could devastate the estuary. It is appropriate to review these threats here. They reflect, as it were, the state of the continuing battle to preserve the Medway Estuary.

It was not until soon after the Second World War that the first major industrial development took place on the Medway, when the British Petroleum oil refinery was constructed on the Isle of Grain, with its associated dock complex for handling oil tankers. The refinery was built on an area of marshland much frequented by white-fronted geese, thus destroying their habitat. Surprisingly, a pool inside the refinery boundary has since proved popular with pochard and is visited at times by Bewick's swans.

The potential menace posed by the refinery is oil pollution. Small spills occur from time to time, but as yet the *Seestern* spill in September 1966 has been the only incident to qualify as a disaster.

This was studied in detail over the subsequent sixteen months (Harrison and Buck 1967). Briefly, 1,700 tons of light oil were

38. Looking north across the Medway mud to the Isle of Grain refinery. It was from there that the *Seestern* pollution originated in 1966.

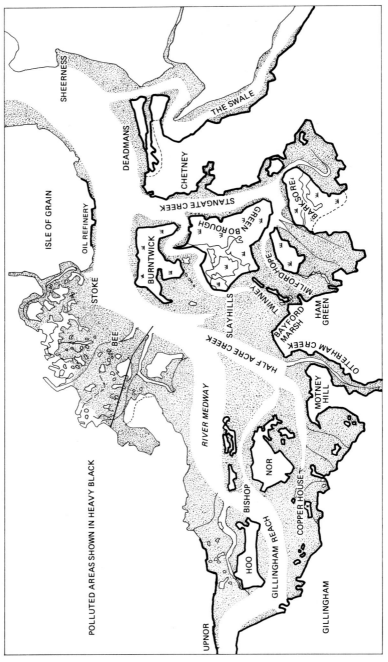

Figure 5. Medway Estuary oil pollution 1966.

124

discharged into the estuary at night on a big flood tide, instead of into the refinery. The oil was swept rapidly into the Medway basin and for the next thirty-six hours, driven by tides and north-east winds, a vast sheet of oil was swept around the southern side and extended twenty-one miles inland. About 8,000 acres of saltmarsh were polluted and great stretches of the intertidal zone. (Fig. 5.)

The master of the *Seestern* was later fined £750 under the Oil in Navigable Waters Act, 1955, and claims then made against the owners, for damage to such things as boats and jetties, totalled £27,000.

It is regrettable that there can be no compensation in law for damage to wildlife, for at least 5,000 birds were estimated to have died of oiling. Fortunately, at that time, the wildfowl population was at a low point and only thirty-six mallard, twenty mute swans, two pochard, a pintail, shelduck and red-breasted merganser were picked up dead. Had it been mid-winter, it would have been far worse.

As it was, wildfowl were far more seriously affected by the cleansing operation organised by the Medway Conservancy Board after consultation with all interests concerned, including naturalists and wildfowlers. At that time, we did not fully appreciate the devastating effects of detergents on the whole marine ecosystem and we all agreed to its use. In all, 6,200 gallons of detergent (Gamlen and BP 1002 Oil Spill Remover) were used.

By mid-October, all the green seaweeds had turned brown, withered and died. The mollusc, laver spire shell, was decimated. A fantastic bank of dead ones, washed ashore on Milfordhope, was estimated to contain 120 million shells, while large numbers of ragworms, shore crabs, common mussels and flounders were killed. Shrimps and dover soles completely disappeared.

On the higher saltings where the oil had been carried by the big tides, the plants were coated with oil and died. This resulted in accelerated tidal erosion of the saltings.

By early 1967, molluscs were recolonising the intertidal zone; by the spring it was hard to realise that anything had happened and in the summer there was a profuse growth of green seaweeds. It was as if the estuary had been fertilised and this in fact may well have happened with a breakdown of the oil.

The results on certain wildfowl species within the two study areas – Half Acre Creek and around Greenborough and Milfordhope Islands, are set out in table 20.

Table 20:

A statistical analysis of the major wildfowl population changes following oil pollution of the Medway Estuary in September 1966

Half Acre Creek (Oct.–Dec. inclusive)

Species	Peak Counts Mean 1961–65 (Max.-Min.)	1966	1967	Standard Deviation $\frac{Range}{6}$	Co-efficient of Variation	Changes expressed as % of 1961–65 Mean		
						1961–65 to 1966	1966 to 1967	1961–65 to 1967
Goldeneye	25(30–9)	20	33	35	14	−20	+52	+32
Shelduck	314(600–120)	13	620	80	25	−96	+193	+97
Brent goose	57(90–40)	8	30	8	14	−86	+39	+47
Greenborough-Milfordhope (Oct.–Dec. inclusive)								
Wigeon	1400(2200–800)	1000	2500	233	17	−29	+107	+79
Pintail	100(250–27)	75	250	37	37	−25	+175	+150
Shelduck	300(600–150)	150	400	75	25	−50	+83	+33
Brent goose	82(150–40)	17	80	15	18	−95	+245	+150

These results have been submitted to a statistical assessment and the changes found can be arranged in order of significance. For 1966 the decreases were as follows:

	Greenborough-Milfordhope	Half Acre Creek
No significant change	Wigeon Pintail	Goldeneye
Significant fall at 5% level	Shelduck	—
Significant fall at 1% level	Brent goose	Shelduck Brent goose

In 1967, the same rearrangement demonstrates the recovery:

	Greenborough-Milfordhope	Half Acre Creek
Significant rise at 5% level	—	Brent goose
Significant rise at 1% level	Wigeon Pintail Shelduck Brent goose	Goldeneye Shelduck

These results show the serious effect of the loss of intertidal marine fauna on the two most dependent species – brent goose and shelduck. Goldeneye and the two dabbling species pintail and wigeon were unaffected. The two dabblers were able to turn to the brackish marshes. The recovery in 1967, however, was remarkable for the increase observed in all five species.

The inescapable conclusion to be learned from the *Seestern* disaster was that the use of detergent was utterly wrong and unnecessary. Nevertheless, this did not stop an estimated £5,000,000 being wasted on detergent later when the *Torrey Canyon* broke up (Maxwell and Baker 1967). It is now accepted policy only to use detergent on beaches which are of the greatest aesthetic and recreational value.

The next major industrial development on the Medway was the construction of the coal or oil burning 2000 megawatt power station at Kingsnorth at the western end of Stoke Saltings, built on 400 acres of excellent brackish marshland at the head of Damhead Creek between 1963 and 1967.

The construction of Kingsnorth is an example of an industrial development which has not proved adverse to wildfowl, indeed the reverse has happened. Two lagoons, destined for settling ash when

127

coal is being burned, were constructed just to the east and the tanker terminal off Oakham Ness was connected to the mainland by a jetty. This resulted in the formation of a beautifully sheltered bay to the west of Oakham Island bordering Slede Ooze (given to the Mayor of Rochester by George II to improve the oyster fishery).

The result of this additional shelter and lack of disturbance was a marked increase in wildfowl as shown in the following table.

Table 21: *Peak wildfowl counts at Kingsnorth, 1951–74*

	1951–61	1962–67	1968–74
Mallard	50	250	2000
Teal	100	300	1400
Wigeon	150	1000	1100
Pintail	—	200	1250
Shelduck	150	500	950

In addition, up to 120 shoveler, 155 tufted duck, 130 pochard and small numbers of scaup, red-breasted mergansers, eider and brent have been seen in recent years. Gadwall, shoveler, pochard, tufted duck, shelduck and mallard have all bred on the lagoons and both wigeon and pintail have been seen in summer.

By agreement with the CEGB, Kingsnorth became a joint reserve of the Kent Wildfowlers' Association and WAGBI in 1968. No one would claim that these remarkable increases were solely the result of the increased security and shelter at Kingsnorth. They were, of course, a reflection of the increases on the estuary as a whole, but the new shelter was there to be used and indeed it was.

With the increasing use now being made of coal rather than oil, the lagoons with their islands and reed beds are changing to their true function as ash-settling lagoons and this in turn will result in a change-over from wildfowl to wading birds as prime users, but the Oakham duck roost will be unaffected and should be as good as ever.

This is not to say that we would ever advocate a mass of new power stations as a method of habitat improvement! Circumstances at Kingsnorth have inadvertently proved ideal and wildlife conservation should now always be thought of at the planning stage of any power station.

The next power station, at present in construction on the Isle of Grain, will not have lagoons, and unfortunately a power line linking Kingsnorth to Grain now runs beside Stoke fleet and although the earth wire (into which birds fly) has been marked, wildfowl are still being killed by it.

Furthermore, the power line from Grain, after running under the mouth of the Medway, will come out on the tip of Chetney and pylons will carry the cable right through the heart of the peninsula. This is a potentially most serious threat which will be watched, but it is the greatest pity that all the pleas put forward at the public enquiry for the proposed line to be shifted to the eastern edge of the peninsula, or better still along the far side of the Swale, could not be implemented and thus a major Medway flight line avoided.

The most serious threat of all (so far) had a happier outcome. This was in relation to a possible Maritime Industrial Development Area (MIDA), for which the Medway was short-listed with two other prime sites (North Humberside and North Severn Estuary) in 1968 by the National Ports Council.

A MIDA has been described as 'a very large port for very large ships drawing a great deal of water, surrounded by a very great deal of primary industry using what comes out of the ships, and a very great deal of secondary industry using what comes out of the primary industry.' Just what this means may be assessed from the following hypothetical industrial package for 1986 used as a basis for calculations in the Economist Intelligence Unit Report on the Medway: 'Two oil refineries, two petrochemical plants, one steel works, one aluminium smelter, two paper mills, one fertilizer plant, one container port, one rail marshalling yard and twenty-two plants of various sizes in ancillary industry.'

Little wonder that those concerned with the future well-being of the estuary and all its different amenities were aghast when this came into the open, and we discovered that the entire southern side of the estuary would be destroyed, as would a large part of the Kentish countryside lying to the south, the site of a new town to house the people.

The MIDA threat did a fine service, for it catalysed us all into great activity to produce the data needed to put forward the case for the Medway's conservation. The Nature Conservancy set up a working party under the Chairmanship of Dr Bryn Green, which produced a most important Report, *Wildlife Conservation in the North Kent Marshes*. In advance of this, the Medway Preservation Society's Report *The Effects of a Maritime Industrial Development Area on the Medway Estuary* constituted the strongest possible reaction to the Kent County Council's Report *The Potential of the Medway Estuary as a Maritime Industrial Development Area.* WAGBI then produced a more specialised publication *Wildfowl of the North Kent Marshes*, followed by a joint Kent Ornithological Society – WAGBI publication, *Breeding Birds of the Medway Estuary*.

The public alarm about a possible Medway MIDA was very considerable; the conservation case unanswerable. One wondered what was the point of the Countryside Commission's *Special Report on Coastal Preservation and Development* (1970) which recognised the special scientific importance of the North Kent Marshes and the Government's *Strategic Plan for the South-East* (1970) which designated these marshes as an 'Area of Significant Environmental Resources'.

The whole problem was discussed at the Ramsar International Conference in February 1971 and at last one saw the real value of all the wildfowl counts which had been made over the years, for John Anderton, WAGBI's Director and a non-Governmental member of the British delegation, was able to put forward the most authoritative conservation case.

The Conference unanimously adopted a special Recommendation addressed to the British Government which for the first time brought home to the Authorities the international implications of the proposed desecration of the South Medway. The following is the text:

RECOMMENDATIONS adopted by the International Conference on the Conservation of Wetlands and Waterfowl attended by Delegates and Observers from 23 countries and 8 International Organisations meeting at Ramsar, Iran, 3rd February, 1971.

RECOMMENDATION 5. *Conservation of the Medway Estuary, England*

The Conference,

NOTING that it is proposed that the Medway Estuary in Kent, England, be considered for development as a Maritime Industrial Development Area (MIDA);

TAKING INTO CONSIDERATION THAT THE area is of outstanding International importance to migratory waterfowl and could well become critically important as a wintering ground for part of the fifth of the world population of the dark-bellied race of the Brent goose, *Branta bernicla*, that would be displaced if Foulness became the site for London's third airport or a 'Europort' dock complex;

RECOMMENDS
That the United Kingdom Government exclude this vitally important area from such development projects.

In 1974, the Kent County Council in a further and most welcome report, recognised the prime conservation interest on the south side of the Medway Estuary and recommended that this area 'should be kept open and restricted to nature conservation with compatible recreational use.' This report gave rise to tremendous relief.

One now has to guard against piecemeal development which may be even more difficult – a rumoured hoverport on the north shore; further dock installations within the estuary and so on. The Medway of course has a long and famous history in this respect with the Royal Naval Dockyard at Chatham, where the first big warship, the 184-gun *Great Harry* was built in 1488. Nelson's Flagship, *HMS Victory* was also built at Chatham in 1765. Sir Francis Drake's father, the Reverend Edmund Drake, was the vicar of Upchurch and the family lived on a Medway barge where the young Francis was perhaps inspired to join the Navy by seeing the warships moving in and out of Chatham – so in reality, Drake he was a Kentish man!

Not all the naval associations of the Medway have been happy ones, for it was in June 1667 that the Dutch fleet under Admiral de Ruyter sailed up the Estuary to burn the British fleet just up-river from Kingsnorth, successfully unlocking the chain which was stretched across the main channel between Darnet and Hoo.

In the two world wars it was of course one of the three Home Ports of the Royal Navy and the Headquarters of the Commander-in-Chief, The Nore, and as such played a major role in the war at sea. Now warships have largely given way to merchantmen, although an occasional nuclear submarine can be seen, but it is the Medway Ports Authority which now looks to the future of the Medway as a port and is facing the problem of expansion. Fortunately their ideas seem to be to develop Sheerness, another naval dockyard now closed, and to construct new docks on Lappel Bank to the immediate south, on the east bank of the Swale. This development is ideally situated to do no harm to the environment.

An excellent example of what we mean by 'piecemeal development' was reported in the *International Freighting Weekly* No. 302 of 4th February, 1976 under the banner headline *Massive plan for Medway Dock Complex.* It went on to say:

'Plans for a massive dock complex in the Sheerness area – possibly covering up to 1,000 acres – are, it is understood, now being prepared by a subsidiary of the Bowater Paper Group.

'The new dock complex is likely to be located on the western shore of the mouth of the Medway, probably on the south coast of the Isle of Grain.

131

'Another site on the north-east corner of Chetney Marshes off the southern shore of the Medway Estuary has also been considered.

'The port plan has been a well kept secret – even the Medway Port Authority is unaware of the project.'

One can only hope that such a ruinous plan will never materialise. Ironically enough, its publication came at the very moment to dampen our elation over the results of the latest mid-January wildfowl counts on the Medway Estuary, when the new record total of 21,500 wildfowl had just been found. Such is the lot of the wildfowl conservationist!

Some Medway saltmarshes have from time to time been reclaimed for agriculture. In general, these reclaimed marshes with their fleet systems fringed with beds of sea club rush and rough grazing land are much better nesting areas for wildfowl than are saltmarshes with their risks of tidal inundation. Duckling survival is better too.

Chetney – the ending 'ey' being derived from the Saxon to indicate a marshy place – was already being reclaimed by the close of the sixteenth century and when surveyed in 1968–69 was found to be supporting eighty-nine pairs of mallard, thirty-two pairs of shelduck, seven pairs of pochard, three pairs of garganey, two pairs of tufted duck and of teal and one pair of gadwall. Reclamation had therefore produced the most important wildfowl nesting area on the estuary in association with intensive grazing by sheep and cattle, the 1,200 acres surveyed supporting 2,800 head of stock in summer.

In 1872, George Webb of Tunstall carried out the prodigious task of reclaiming both Greenborough and Milfordhope islands – 382 acres being successfully enclosed at a cost of £28,000 – but his success was short-lived, for a high tide wrecked the walls on 31st December, 1904.

In the early 1960's, Bill and Harry Mouland successfully reclaimed Barksore on the south shore of the estuary and much of this has now been ploughed and sown and is being grazed by sheep. In 1972, when this area was surveyed it held twenty-eight pairs of mallard, twenty-two pairs of shelduck, four pairs of shoveler, three pairs of greylag geese, two pairs of teal and pochard and a pair of wigeon. It was here that the first pair of black-tailed godwits to rear young in Kent bred in 1972.

Duck were nesting in the cover of hastate orache, much of which has now been removed, and there is now a definite lack of nesting cover, which could easily be rectified without detriment to the farming. There is considerable scope for a most interesting experiment in management here.

132

39. A typical freshmarsh fleet on Chetney.

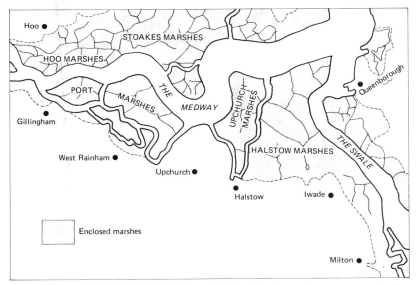

Figure 6. The Medway Estuary 1769, showing the extent of the reclamation by the Romans.

40. Barksore marsh on the left was reclaimed after the main channel was blocked with old concrete barges.

It is sad to close this account of the Medway on yet another worrying note, but that is the all-too familiar lot of those concerned with wetland conservation. Just as things were looking so much more hopeful for the south shore, the Public Services Committee of the Greater London Council began considering a plan in 1972 to embank the entire remaining unspoilt saltings on the north shore – 1,600 acres of Stoke Ooze, lying between the Grain oil refinery and Kingsworth power station, thus totally destroying the north shore.

The entire site would be raised twenty feet by tipping 20 million tons of London's refuse, sections of land being redeveloped when ready. The whole project seems quite monstrous, particularly when it is likely that the cost of the scheme will be comparable to alternative and far more socially acceptable methods of disposal such as incineration.

Meanwhile in any feasibility tests, it will be vital to know what effect this dreadful scheme will have on the remainder of the estuary if the whole of the northern shore was ever to be embanked. The changed tidal flow could well cause marked changes and increased erosion on the south shore and the islands.

AN AREA OF INTERNATIONAL IMPORTANCE

On the conservation side, one need only say that the prime interest ornithologically on Stoke is in the breeding season, where the maze of small islands makes the area the finest nesting grounds on the estuary. Of the total of 5,527 pairs of wildfowl, waders, rails, terns and gulls found nesting on the 1972 Medway Estuary Survey no less than 4,839 pairs were nesting here – 87·4 per cent of the total.

Quite apart from this, the whole amenity value of the Medway is at stake, and the GLC must expect the united opposition of everyone who enjoys the estuary and a desperate fight from those who live in the surrounding towns and villages.

THE THAMES

The flat marshlands which extend for about fourteen miles all the way along the northern side of the Hundred of Hoo from Higham to Grain, reach up to three miles inland at Cooling and cover about twenty square miles. This delightful area is overlooked by Cooling Castle, enlarged as a defence against the French in the late fourteenth century by Lord Cobham.

The atmosphere of these marshes and the tidal flats beyond the distant sea wall is delightfully unspoilt and wild and it is unfortunate that such areas should over the ages have come to be regarded almost with dread and superstition by so many people. This is, of course, quite understandable when one thinks of the thirteen little tombstones just along the lane from Cooling Castle. Dickens wrote of Pip in *Great Expectations* finding out 'that the dark flat wilderness beyond the churchyard, intersected with dykes and mounds and gates, with scattered cattle feeding on it, was the marshes; and that the lower leaden line beyond which the wind was rushing, was the sea.' Needless to say, the atmosphere in the film version was bleak in the extreme with splendid banks of mist and so on!

From time to time that same sea, backed by violent gales from the north-west, has resulted in surge tides which have wrought terrible loss of life, both to humans and farm animals, when all the marshes have been flooded. One of the first to be chronicled was on 16th February, 1735; another occurred in November 1897 and the last (which nearly trapped both JGH and PFH on the Isle of Sheppey) took place on the night of 31st January, 1953. As we came off the island that night we saw the sea walls giving way around us – a terrifying experience.

135

Little wonder, then, that it is so difficult to convince many people that wetlands are not wastelands, fit only for refuse tips and reclamation, for this view is almost inbred in so many of us by centuries of fear and abhorrence of such places.

As a result of the 1953 surge tide, the height of the seawalls throughout the area was raised and the two main areas of Thames salting in Egypt and St Mary's Bays were enclosed by a new outer seawall.

Yantlet creek, used as a channel for shipping linking the Thames and Medway, until the time of Edward III, when it became too silted, was also embanked after 1953 and is now, like the other former channels along the Thames, a beautiful reed-fringed fleet.

At the western end of the peninsula, a number of large lagoons were created on Cliffe marshes where industrial clay was being extracted. The first pit was flooded in 1935 and this new habitat became a paradise for waterfowl, particularly diving duck and a fine roost for swans. For the past ten years these pools have gradually been filled by dredgings pumped in from the Thames, and their heyday is now past.

The principal worry on the Thames freshmarshes has focused recently on changing trends in agricultural use, from the traditional high water table and grazing by sheep and cattle to cereal and potato growing, which requires a significantly lower water table.

41. Cliffe Pools. From the air the old tidal creeks, long since enclosed by the sea wall, can still be seen clearly.

The botanical picture of the Thames freshmarshes (as well as those on Chetney and the Isle of Sheppey) is comparatively simple. In many places these freshmarshes lie appreciably below the level of the normal high tide mark, having presumably dried out and lowered since the time when they were first embanked, so that the strength of the seawalls and the state of their sluice gates are vital. In some areas (particularly on Chetney) there is a gradation of salinity from the saltmarsh immediately outside the seawall, through the brackish water zone on the inside to drier freshwater areas further inland.

The pastures behind the seawall have a number of grass species, namely seameadow grass, sea barley, reflexed saltmarsh grass, sea couch and marsh foxtail. The fleets and ditches support a profuse growth of fennel-leaved pondweed, hornwort, milfoil and, further inland, water crowfoot. They are fringed by extensive beds of sea club rush, glaucous bulrush, spike-rush, Norfolk reed and mare's tail. With the exception of Norfolk reed, all of these are valuable duck foods and all the reeds provide vital cover.

In wet winters many low lying areas become flooded and these floods are much favoured by the wigeon and white-fronted goose and in spring by shoveler and shelduck and the early garganey.

The international importance of the Thames as assessed by George Atkinson-Willes from his international counts 1967–73 is only for shelduck, although both wigeon and shoveler easily come into this category in good seasons. It is also (coupled with the Swale) one of the three main areas in Britain for wintering European white-fronted geese – the others being on the New Grounds at the Wildfowl Trust's Slimbridge headquarters and on the Hampshire Avon.

At low water the mudflats of Blythe and Roas Banks are uncovered for about a mile outwards from the sea wall, except at Lower Hope Point where the deep water channel comes close to the Kentish shore and where sea duck, particularly common scoters, can sometimes be seen in some numbers. The mudflats support vast numbers of laver spire shell, this mollusc being the main shelduck food, and they also provide for the roosting requirements of the white-fronted geese.

After the sea wall was strengthened following the 1953 surge tide – which resulted in an attractive new 'borrow dyke' along the inside, much favoured by nesting pochard and tufted duck – the farmers have felt secure enough to contemplate arable farming, particularly now that the economics of meat production have rendered the old traditional farming so much less profitable. It is little wonder that significant areas of both the Thames and Sheppey marshes have been tile-drained, ploughed and turned over to cereal production.

It is regrettable that whereas there are very substantial grants available to farmers through their Ministry to encourage drainage schemes, there should be no comparable 'conservation grant' which could be made available through the Department of the Environment to save particularly valuable areas such as grazing marshes which frequently flood, although perhaps the controversy over London's third airport at Foulness has now set the precedent for this.

In view of the almost total lack of factual information on the ornithological and botanical changes likely to occur as the result of tile drainage schemes, it was agreed to undertake a survey on a 'before-and-after' basis, and 300 acres of Cooling marsh farmed by Ronald and Duncan Maclean, both keen wildfowler-conservationists, were selected for this study in January 1974, when their application to tile drain was received.

A meeting was held with the farmers, attended by Mr A. B. Trask, the Divisional Surveyor of the Ministry of Agriculture, officials of the Nature Conservancy Council's South-East Region and ourselves.

The meeting was most successful. We believe it was the first such meeting ever held between 'drainers and conservationists', and, much to everyone's surprise, we found that we achieved a great

43, 44 & 45. Opposite left, widening a
: with a dragline to reverse the plant
:ession. Top, deepening a ditch before the
:ning begins. Farmers in the area are co-
rating. Centre, improving wildfowl
:tat with explosives. Right, a garganey's
: in a crop of wheat on newly drained
. The duck has soiled the eggs on leaving
nest. This is thought to be done to keep
:redators.

deal. It was agreed that the three main fleets would be maintained with water levels at their pre-drainage height and a branch of one of them – Salt Fleet – destined to be infilled, would be left as it was.

Those dykes selected for retention, deepening and widening, would not be straightened, but would remain sinuous, thus maintaining the number of shoreline territories for duck.

Ploughing and tile draining would not take place within about ten metres of the present fleet margins and the new dykes would be twenty-one feet wide and six feet deep, thus ensuring relatively gentle sloping banks. Herbicides would not be used for cleaning purposes.

Finally the Macleans agreed to give sympathetic consideration to holding water at a high level on two pasture areas to the west for wintering and, if possible, breeding wildfowl.

A neighbouring farmer, Tim Long, another enthusiastic wildfowler-conservationist, has also carried out extensive improvements in Hope Fleet along the southern boundary of the study area, clearing and creating new stretches of open water by dragline and explosives and building embankments on the fields for shallow stretches of flood water to compensate for those areas he had tile-drained earlier for cereals.

As yet, the study is incomplete, but in the dry spring of 1974, when the area was still heavily grazed, there was little nesting cover. Next spring was exceptionally wet, with plenty of standing water, not only on the grazing lands, but also in the sprouting wheat in spite of the tile-drainage. This was undoubtedly an encouragement for shoveler to stay and nest. Furthermore there was excellent nesting cover in the growing wheat, where the dabbling duck nests were all found.

Table 22: *Estimated number of pairs of wildfowl (with totals of nests or broods shown in brackets) in the Thames study area.*

	1974 (grassland)	1975 (cereals)
Mallard	16 (9)	26 (18)
Teal	—	1 (1)
Gadwall	1 (1)	1
Garganey	2 (1)	4 (4)
Shoveler	3 (1)	15 (12)
Pochard	12 (11)	12 (4)
Tufted duck	2	3 (3)
Mute swan	6 (4)	5 (4)
Total pairs:	40	67

It is interesting to note that the diving duck increased by one pair, which is well in keeping with the unchanged water levels in the fleets. Dabbling duck, however, showed a fifty-three per cent increase, which was partly due to the improved cover provided by the growing wheat and partly to the wet spring which encouraged shoveler and garganey to breed. In the census, it was striking how the ducks' nests were found in close proximity to flooded spots in the growing wheat.

Of the six other predominant species nesting in either grazing land or winter wheat, the changes from the heavily sheep-grazed grass in 1974 to the growing wheat in 1975 were marked and only one of which, the lapwing, showed a substantial decrease, the other five all increasing considerably.

Table 23: *Other breeding pairs in the Thames study area.*

Species	1974	1975
Redshank	20	37
Lapwing	26	4
Partridge	3	19
Skylark	118	210
Yellow wagtail	18	78
Meadow pipit	13	71

One other remarkable happening has been the occurrence in the past two springs of small numbers of dotterel, which appear to have been attracted to the newly-turned soil. It is possible that these birds are linked with the population now summering below sea level in the new Dutch polders.

In the autumn of 1975, up to 1,500 mallard were flighting to the wheat stubbles in the study area. This census was repeated in 1976 which was a drought spring. But it still seems that the growing wheat provides better nesting cover than close cropped grass, as indeed would be expected. The census will be repeated in 1977, hoping for a normal spring.

It was noticeable in the preceding winter that the growing wheat was being grazed by duck and geese in good numbers – up to 400 white-fronts, 200 pintail and 400 wigeon in February, the wheat being grazed for up to thirty yards out from the edge of the fleets. At the same time teal were finding the new drainage ditches very much to their liking. In late November, 1974, one of Tim Long's flooded areas was most successful, holding 1,000 teal, 200 pintail and sixty wigeon.

141

46. An unexpected visitor to the study area was this dotterel.

In the winter of 1975/76 the combination of the growing wheat and the nearby flooded areas again attracted up to 600 wigeon in the New Year, 350 white-fronted geese and as a new feature, about forty Russian brent geese. On 24th February, the first tundra bean geese to be found in North Kent (three) were identified by Sir Peter Scott when being shown the study area by JGH.

At present it appears that the ideal management of these marshes is a combination of traditional sheep and cattle grazing and cereals, the latter, if properly planned, providing both shoreline territories and good nesting cover and the former excellent grazing and bathing facilities in winter. It could be a very different story if the whole area was to be converted to cereals.

So, for the present we are optimistic as regards agriculture. We also recognise the prime need to produce our own food in this country and that the farmer must expect a reasonable return to his labours. The farmer, in fact, holds the key for the future of wildlife conservation in this overcrowded island and we believe that our combined efforts on the Thames have already shown the real benefits of co-operation.

Two other problems loom large on the Thames at present. The first is a proposed new oil refinery for Burmah Total on Cliffe

142

marshes, a proposal which seems perhaps somewhat curious in the present state of our economy and the diminished use of oil.

In granting planning permission for this refinery early in 1976, the Minister of the Environment over-rode his own Inspectors after two public inquiries, rejected the representations of the Borough and County planning authorities and all the local amenity and conservation organisations. All the evidence indicated that we have adequate refining capacity both nationally and regionally for the foreseeable future, while our refineries are at present working well below their maximum output.

Surely the Minister of the Environment should recognise the immense ecological value of these marshes, the last remaining unspoiled stretch of the south Thames below London.

Another worrying proposal has been made by the Port of London Authority in September 1975 to allow the Greater London Council to deposit river dredgings on PLA land covering an extensive area of Cliffe marshes adjoining Cliffe Fleet along most of its length. Cliffe Fleet is now the main early autumn duck roost on the Thames (2,000 mallard, 400 shoveler and 300 teal in autumn 1975).

The ultimate end of this development would be a scrubland and a stepping stone on the way to the industrialisation of Cliffe marshes in the one area where the deep water channel comes close to the Kent shore. With industry at either end of the Thames marshes at Cliffe and Grain, it is but a short step to the ultimate destruction of the whole area. That is what we fear will come to pass, but even if industry does not materialise, the transformation of Cliffe marshes into scrubland will be enough to ruin that area for wildfowl and quite possibly to render the remaining unspoilt area too small for white-fronted geese.

THE SWALE

The Swale Channel separates the Isle of Sheppey from the mainland and extends from Queenborough in the west, where it joins the Medway, to Shellness in the east, where it joins the North Sea off Whitstable Bay. The western third is only about a quarter of a mile wide, but the channel is used by vessels coming to Ridham Dock, just east of Kingsferry bridge, carrying timber for Bowater's paper mills at Kemsley near Sittingbourne.

The eastern two-thirds of the Swale are considerably shallower and wider, mostly about a mile wide at full tide, but twice as wide off Shellness. Extensive mud and sandbanks are uncovered at low tide

47. The western end of the Swale with Deadman's Island in the foreground and the Kingsferry bridge in the distance.

and a famous shell and shingle spit has formed at Shellness (smaller ones are found at Allhallows, Grain, Hoo, Deadman's, Leysdown and Seasalter).

Three creeks run southwards into Kent – Milton, Conyer and Faversham Creeks – while the main one on the Sheppey side, Windmill Creek, which separated Elmley and Harty 'Islands' was walled off after the 1953 surge tide close to its mouth at Spitend Point.

One big island – Fowley – on the south side, close to Teynham Levels, was formerly an important nesting area, particularly for terns, before brown rats caused the birds to move across to Flanders Mere, close to the old mouth of Windmill Creek.

The eastern end of the Swale is a particularly important area to the conservationist. On the north, Shellness is one of the best examples in the country of a coastal spit, ridge and dune system, based on shells (mainly cockles), shell sands and shingle, with a characteristic hooked tip caused by tidal drift. This encloses a fine area of saltmarsh with good cover of cordgrass, much favoured by mallard when it is too rough at sea in their normal roosting area. Shellness itself is used as a wader roost and the wide mouth of the Swale is the

144

best area in North Kent for seeing marine duck, particularly during and after north-west gales.

On the south shore, off Castle Coot, eel-grass has regenerated well and these flats are the main haunt of brent geese on the Swale.

Over the past twenty years, fears have increased about the pollution of the Swale by effluent from Kemsley Mills and discharges of wood pulp have been recorded as being carried as far east as Whitstable. No evidence could be produced of any decrease in wildfowl clearly related to this pollution, the only marine duck definitely to show a decrease being the red-breasted merganser, but this is general throughout the North Kent Marshes.

However, a new effluent treatment plant has recently been constructed by Bowaters, which has been urgently needed.

The extensive grazing marshes with their fleet systems along the southern part of the Isle of Sheppey are similar to those on the Thames and provide important feeding grounds for white-fronted geese and wigeon in winter and for nesting wildfowl, particularly pochard in summer. Like the Thames, they are being subjected to drainage for cereal crops.

The Swale is internationally important in the majority of winters for wigeon and shelduck and occasionally for shoveler. It is also a high category of international importance for wading birds, with big flocks of knot, bar-tailed godwit and oystercatcher on the eastern Swale.

A fine area of clay pits at Murston near Sittingbourne is managed by the Kent Trust for Nature Conservation as a reserve and is important for nesting pochard. Gravel excavations near Oare should also become important in the near future.

Formerly there were two working decoys near Sittingbourne on the south-east side of Kingsferry Bridge. One at Grovehurst was constructed about 1706, according to Sir Ralph Payne Gallwey, as a two-acre four pipe decoy. It was not worked after 1866 when the new railway to Sheerness was built close by. The catch ranged from 500 to 2,500 a season, over 1,000 mallard and 1,000 teal having been caught in one season. Others caught included wigeon, pintail, shoveler, pochard, tufted duck and goldeneye. Eventually the pond was filled and planted with fruit trees.

A second decoy was sited close by at Kemsley (now referred to as Grovehurst). This went out of use early in the nineteenth century and was apparently a good decoy for catching teal. The last signs of this decoy, in particular one of its pipes, were destroyed in 1975 when the area was drained for cereals.

145

During the previous decade it had become an important moulting area for up to 150 adult spotted redshank in July and always held duck in small numbers.

THE AMENITIES OF THE NORTH KENT MARSHES

It is only possible to give some indication of the amenity value of this area. Nevertheless, this is a vitally important aspect, for a number of seemingly conflicting interests must be integrated – and with good will and careful planning they can be integrated – with the wildlife interest. There could be no practical future for these marshes if they had to be isolated for wildlife conservation. That would be unthinkable. In the final assessment, the area will be saved by the number of people able to enjoy themselves, coupled with the international and national importance of the marshes for wildlife, which must be maintained and if possible increased.

Sailing

The Medway Preservation Society's report on the effects of a MIDA on the estuary provides the most recent calculations of sailing activities on the Medway and Swale, the Thames being of little significance in this respect because of the extensive mudflats off the seawall.

In 1969 there were no less than 3,718 small craft, both sail and power, in use and it was calculated that no less than 17,500 people were participating in this sport. Since then it is reasonable to assume an increase of about twenty per cent, which means just over 20,000 people – a remarkable figure.

It must be remembered that most of the sailing activities finish by late October, so that disturbance to wintering waterfowl is minimal. In summer, the position is less happy than it need be, due to disturbances from yachtsmen going ashore, particularly on the Medway islands, sometimes with dogs, even with baskets to collect eggs. The majority of waterfowl nesting on these islands use the sea walls to escape high tides and mallard, shelduck and oystercatchers nesting on the walls beside Stangate Creek have all decreased markedly. Picnic litter left by sailing parties inevitably encourages brown rats which in turn predate the nesting birds. Recent dry summers have also seen extensive sea wall fires started by such picnickers, destroying nests and later increasing tidal erosion.

All this could be avoided if sailors would accept a code of conduct

146

under which they will not go ashore, except in emergency, between April and July inclusive, something widely practised in Holland. This is really little to ask and once universally accepted, there should be no conflict between sailing and wildlife in its present state. Indeed we think that boating could be gradually increased if carefully monitored. An important factor here is the need for well organised marinas where moorings should be dependent upon maintaining this code of conduct. Such a code is already being operated by two marinas on the Swale. Marinas should be dredged so as to be accessible at low tide, thus reducing the temptation to go ashore elsewhere, and should be well landscaped.

Disturbances from water ski-ing can be much more serious. Wearing wet suits, enthusiasts are now appearing even in mid-

48. Unless controlled, water skiing is a serious disturbance to birds on the Swale.

winter. However, the Medway Ports Authority has drawn up a Notice to Mariners (No 19 of 1973) indicating the prohibited areas on the Medway and Swale for water ski-ing and aqua-planing, which is now restricted to members of clubs approved by the Harbour Master. This is a great improvement, but there are still a few areas of great importance for waterfowl where restrictions should apply but as yet do not.

Similar restrictions may become necessary for small hovercraft, should these become widespread, for they are noisy and their slipstreams destroy both vegetation and nests as they travel over marshes.

Birdwatching

The North Kent Marshes are a powerful attraction for birdwatchers, and rightly so. Organised field meetings several times a year are arranged by such organisations as the Royal Society for the Protection of Birds, the Kent Ornithological Society, Kent Trust for Nature Conservation, Kent Field Club, the London Natural History Society, London University Natural History Society and a wide range of schools, not to mention a host of individual enthusiasts.

The Kent Trust has had applications for parties of school children filling two or three buses to visit the reserve at Shellness; this is an area where sheer numbers can have a detrimental effect on flora and on nesting birds, so that careful control is necessary. However, on public rights of way along sea walls, such large numbers are virtually harmless, and many birds can be seen and healthy exercise enjoyed. Most of the tracks leading to the sea wall are across farmland, so the Country Code must be carefully obeyed.

Wildfowling

The Nature Conservancy's report *Wildlife Conservation in the North Kent Marshes* made the following statement:

The Wildfowlers' Association of Great Britain and Ireland in conjunction with the Kent Wildfowlers' Association carries out a number of research studies in the Medway Estuary, some of which have provided much practical information to the wildfowler and ornithologist. These have included a duck production survey in which sex and age ratio figures are obtained from the wings of shot duck saved by wildfowlers, and food studies based on viscera analyses which have led to a basic understanding of the feeding habits and requirements of all the quarry species of duck. The production study is still in progress. Carefully controlled introductions of greylag geese on the 2,000 acre Chetney WAGBI Reserve are being made to discover if it is possible to alter the flyway of Western European greylags between Scandinavia and Spain and divert more to South-East England, and experimental work designed to encourage a breeding population of teal is being carried out with decoy-caught birds.

Organised wildfowling carried out by responsible guns who are normally members of WAGBI or the KWA probably has a negligible effect on the general wildfowl population both in terms of birds killed and the disturbance created. Responsible wildfowling, like fishing, is a controlled exploitation of a resource, and as such very much part and parcel of wildlife conservation. Indeed both the WAGBI and the KWA maintain reserves in the North Kent Marshes. Knowledge of wildfowl populations stems in a considerable part from their researches. Some irresponsible shooters, or 'Marsh Cowboys', however, tend to shoot at almost anything, ignoring the protection afforded to some species and also rights of access to land. Such activity can lead to over-shooting with damaging effects on bird populations principally due to disturbance. Control over this kind of activity is desirable and could be achieved in some areas of special vulnerability by the imposition of byelaws if a suitable statutory framework for the North Kent Marshes were achieved. It is noteworthy that in the Medway where wildfowling is now controlled by the Kent Wildfowlers' Association and private syndicates, large increases in wildfowl populations have occurred.

The Kent Wildfowlers' Association (an affiliated WAGBI Club) has now established four reserves around the Medway, at Kingsnorth Power Station (jointly with WAGBI and the KOS) which occasionally holds up to 5,000 duck; at Motney Hill, where up to 1,000 duck have been counted; Captain's Pool inside the Isle of Grain Refinery, a haunt of Bewick's swans, and their most recent acquisition, the embanked section of Yantlet Creek, now a fleet holding well in excess of 1,000 duck at times in winter and an important breeding area.

Apart from this, the KWA holds extensive shooting rights, which include the Thames foreshore just east of Cliffe Fleet to Yantlet, Nor Island and Stoke Saltings on the Medway. Syndicates within the KWA shoot some of the freshmarshes and on the opening day all shooting stops at 10 am and from then on there is no further shooting until 1st October, thus ensuring that the home-bred mallard are not overshot.

Without doubt, wardening by wildfowlers is solving the problem of the 'Marsh Cowboy'; predators – crows, rats and foxes – are controlled and in the event of prolonged severe weather, it is WAGBI policy to apply a voluntary ban on wildfowling.

Wildfowlers play a vital part in obtaining counts from virtually the

whole of the Medway Estuary, including the islands, and the KWA
cooperates closely with the Kent Ornithological Society in the
Medway nesting censuses.

Angling

Commercial fishing by small inshore trawlers is on the increase and
it is important for other water users to give way to the trawlers while
they are working. Amateur sea anglers, often commercially
organised in launches, have at present a rather bad name caused by a
thoughtless few anchoring in fairways, even occasionally mooring to
navigational buoys, which is illegal. An oyster fishery is now being
re-established in Stangage Creek.

Disturbances from bait diggers can at times prove excessive – up
to 160 people have been counted at work in Whistable Bay at one
time.

Archaeology

Archaeologists have long studied the North Kent Marshes,
particularly the Medway Estuary with its famous Roman
associations. Their researches did little damage, but achieved much.
More recently, with the newly found interest in Victoriana, a
number of people not worthy of being described as archaeologists
have appeared on the saltmarshes, particularly on the Medway,
where certain islands were reclaimed at the end of the nineteenth
century, and have dug deep into causeways and sea walls. They
make no effort to refill their holes, so that erosion occurs and the
holes ultimately become filled with silt, which can easily trap
someone, perhaps putting them in danger.

Obviously, with recreational activities of all kinds growing, there
can easily be a clash of interests, often arising through
thoughtlessness or genuine ignorance. The Medway Preservation
Society is presently involved in working out a code of conduct with
the idea of preventing many of these problems before they arise.

Reserves

Apart from those reserves already mentioned under 'Wildfowling',
there are a number of most important reserves on the North Kent

Marshes, including two National Nature Reserves. The first covers 130 acres of mixed woodland at Northward Hill, High Halstow, overlooking the Thames. This holds the largest heronry in Europe and was formerly an important nesting area for duck, including shelduck nesting under brambles, but suitable ground cover has died back over the past twenty-five years; this may regenerate in parts following the ravages of Dutch elm disease.

A second National Nature Reserve was established in 1975 at the eastern end of the Isle of Sheppey consisting of 250 acres of typical grazing marsh and fleets with some saltmarsh, while the Royal Society for the Protection of Birds also established a similar reserve on Elmley Marshes.

A local Nature Reserve of 1,500 acres of the South Swale between Seasalter and Faversham Creek was designated by the County Council in 1969, including the most important eel-grass beds. This is managed by the Kent Trust for Nature Conservation.

Sites of Special Scientific Interest designated under the National Parks Act, 1949, include the Swale (16,780 acres), Chetney (2,300 acres), Yantlet/Stoke Saltings (4,075 acres), High Halstow Marshes

49. Evening on the river; the Medway Estuary off Oakham Island.

THE NORTH KENT MARSHES AND THE SOUTH ESSEX SHORE

(3,200 acres) and Higham Marshes (880 acres). Such sites are of course in no way safeguarded, other than by the planning authority being bound to consult the Nature Conservancy Council before granting permission for any development application. They are some indication of the value of the areas which lack any safeguard. It should also be noted that the most important area of all, the islands in the south-east quadrant of the Medway Estuary, lack even this fragile safeguard.

Clearly what is urgently needed now is some kind of statutory safeguard for the whole of the North Kent Marshes, such as National Park status.

50. Wetlands are not wastelands! Funton Creek, Medway Estuary.

CHAPTER 6

THE WILDFOWL OF THE NORTH KENT MARSHES

W HERE possible, in the sections on the North Kent Marshes and the south Essex coast, wildfowl counts have been analysed by the method evolved by George Atkinson-Willes in his famous monograph *Wildfowl in Great Britain*. Thus for ducks, the *regular* population is from the average of the *three* highest monthly counts. This is in turn averaged over a nummber of seasons, each season extending from August to March. The *maximum* population is the highest single count on record during the season under review. For geese the *average peak* has been used. This consists of the average of the highest single counts for the seasons under review.

In this way, it is possible to compare the decade 1952/61 from the monograph figures with the subsequent fourteen years, divided into two five-year periods and the last four. On the North Kent Marshes, the three areas are considered separately and the Medway figures for the north and south shores have also been separated.

Mute Swan

Without doubt the mute swan is the most neglected of all the wildfowl species in North Kent and this makes it impossible to give a complete picture of its status and distribution.

In 1950, Gillham and Homes wrote that it bred sparingly, only about six pairs being found along the Thames and a few pairs on Sheppey. Herds of more than ten were exceptional, but one of eighteen was present on Sheppey for a month during severe weather in early 1947.

A survey in 1961 by the Kent Ornithological Society showed a marked increase with forty pairs breeding or in territories, including seventeen by the Thames, fourteen on Sheppey and nine by the

153

Medway, as well as a total of 113 non-breeding birds including a herd of eighteen on Stoke lagoon.

No complete surveys have been made since, but examples of non-breeding birds in summer have included twenty-nine on Capel Fleet in April 1964, thirty-one at Grovehurst in April and forty at Stoke in May 1966; forty-one at Cliffe in July 1972 and ninety-one there in August 1973. Two earlier records from Murston clay pits were of seventy-five in July 1957 and seventy in July 1960, probably at a stage in the plant succession when the submergents were ideal for swans.

Winter gatherings in the past eighteen years have been considerably larger than formerly. In the severe winter of 1962/63, a total of 186 involved eighty-nine at Sheerness, sixty-one in Faversham Creek, twenty at Cliffe and sixteen near Gravesend.

Other high counts include the following: fifty-four at High Halstow in October 1965; fifty-five at Cliffe in January 1966; sixty-four at High Halstow in February 1967 and fifty at Murston a month earlier; forty-one at Cliffe in December 1968 and fifty-two at Allhallows in December 1969. Subsequently there have been seventy-eight at Cliffe in December 1971, seventy-three in December 1972, ninety-six in February 1973 and eighty-six in February 1974.

The possibility of some of these mid-winter concentrations including immigrants of overseas origin has long been considered likely by both Ticehurst and James Harrison. Their presence in south-east England was finally proved by ringing recoveries following the severe winter of 1962/63. These included one ringed on the Medway at Maidstone on 21st February, 1963 and recovered on 1st October, 1966 at Mecklenberg, East Germany.

Immigrant mute swans can often be recognised in the field, because they are wary and easily put to flight, quite distinct in behaviour and appearance from the resident birds, for the immigrants keep their necks erect and their plumage compressed in the manner of other wild swans.

One such bird was seen by JGH on Harty on 17th January, 1953, immediately following a spell of severe north-easterly weather. A number of other apparently wild mute swans have been seen in Kent, particularly in 1963, but all away from the North Kent Marshes until 18th October, 1967, when JGH and W. F. A. Buck found two adults at Grovehurst, showing all the character of wild immigrants. A pair of resident mutes attacked the strangers, swimming towards them with arched necks and their back and wing

154

feathers fanned out to provide a complete contrast in appearance. After twenty minutes of being chased, the two immigrants took off and flew high to the west over the Medway.

The date on which these birds were seen coincided with the time when immigrant mute swans can be seen moving south-west across Schleswig-Holstein from the Baltic, and we were both convinced that the two Grovehurst birds provided the first evidence that immigrant mute swans may occur as genuine autumn migrants.

Bewick's Swan

It is a remarkable fact that both Ticehurst in 1909 and James Harrison in 1953, when writing their *Birds of Kent,* could only report this little swan as one of the rarest of hard weather visitors. In fact prior to 1952, the only records were of several herds of wild swans in the mouth of the Thames in the severe winter of 1871, from which two Bewick's swans were shot, as was another on the Medway Estuary on 22nd January, 1897.

51. Bewick's swans.

The great increases which have taken place since the next record in 1952 are shown in the following table in which it has been possible to estimate the individual numbers present each year with reasonable accuracy:

Table 24: *Number of individual Bewick's swans 1952/74*

	1952	53	54	55	56	57	58	59	60	61	62	63
Medway	—	—	—	—	17	2	—	1	7	—	50	10
Thames	—	4	—	23	30	—	1	12	7	2	34	67
Swale	1	—	—	—	6	—	—	—	—	1	—	2
Total	1	4	—	23	53	2	1	13	14	3	84	79

	1964	65	66	67	68	69	70	71	72	73	74	Total
Medway	—	—	4	22	17	25	19	30	20	15	4	243
Thames	19	4	3	1	22	—	34	8	11	65	11	358
Swale	7	3	12	7	4	8	7	2	10	47	53	170
Total	26	7	19	30	43	33	60	40	41	127	68	771

Table 25: *Monthly occurrences of Bewick's swans 1952/74*

Jan	Feb	Mar	Apr	Oct	Nov	Dec
258	222	113	18	68	91	196

During the decade of 1952–61, the average number of individuals visiting our area annually was $11 \cdot 4$, but in the last thirteen years period it has increased to $50 \cdot 5$. These findings are in keeping with the massive increases which have taken place so spectacularly on the Fenland Washes and at Slimbridge, probably as a direct result of changes which have taken place on their other wintering grounds on the Ijsselmeer in Holland.

So far, the most favoured localities are on Cliffe Pools and Yantlet on the Thames; Stoke Fleet, Captain's Pool and Chetney on the Medway, and Windmill Creek and Murston Clay pits on the Swale. With Cliffe Pools now being back-filled with Thames dredgings and with electric pylons now sited along Yantlet and being constructed across Chetney, both in spite of pleas from wildfowl conservationists for route alterations, the future for Bewick's swans in North Kent could be hazardous. Swans are particularly prone to fatal accidents from flying into power lines.

THE WILDFOWL OF THE NORTH KENT MARSHES

European white-fronted Goose

The first mention of this goose in North Kent was in 1885 when 'A Son of the Marshes' wrote that, 'In severe weather, mixed flights of white-fronted and barnacle geese sometimes passed over our north Kent marshlands and strange confused cries were the result – cries that often filled our superstitious folk with terror.'

In 1934 R. B. Sibson considered the white-front an irregular winter visitor. Gillham and Homes date the onset of more regular visits to the winter of 1939/40, but the maximum did not exceed 200 until 1946/47, when 500 occurred on the Thames, at which time the Sheppey marshes first began to be used.

Since then, a strong tradition has been established for both the Thames and Sheppey marshes. All Kentish birds to date are referable to the European race.

On the Medway, parties of about fifty have been seen almost annually since 1961, occasionally up to 250. These are usually on the move between Sheppey and the Thames, but small flocks sometimes feed regularly on Chetney pastures, roosting on the Medway Estuary.

52. White-fronted geese at Cooling marsh.

Table 26: *The regular and maximum counts of white-fronted geese 1952–75*

		1952–61	1961–71	1971–75
Thames	Regular	500	608	526
	Max	1500	1625	1000
Sheppey	Regular	235	484	511
	Max	630	1120	950
Total of regular counts		735	1092	1037

These figures demonstrate the continuing build-up on the Sheppey marshes and a rather static situation on the Thames.

In his review of the status of this goose in Britain from 1946 to 1969, Malcolm Ogilvie could detect no trends, except perhaps a slight decrease in total peak numbers. The increases in North Kent are therefore encouraging and now only the flocks at Slimbridge and along the Hampshire Avon are substantially larger. As the Kent flocks are the nearest to the main wintering grounds in Holland, it seems probable that the trend of increase in Kent reflects what is happening in Holland, particularly on the new Ijsselmeer polder goose reserves, where the population has almost trebled in the past twenty years. The next really severe winter could well disperse over 100,000 white-fronts from Holland, but in January 1976, when there were two weeks of severe weather, the white-fronts did not undertake any weather migration. Indeed numbers were generally well below average even for a normal winter in England. On the North Kent Marshes it is doubtful if they exceeded 1,000 and one now begins to wonder if the polder goose reserves may not break the tradition for the white-fronts' English haunts.

It is usual for the main influx to occur between late December and mid-January, often, but not necessarily, precipitated by severe weather. Peak counts invariably occur in February, the last big flocks departing in mid-March. Early arrivals may be expected in October, an exceptionally early party of twenty-five being seen on the Thames by Tim Long on 25th September, 1972. An occasional bird lingers into early April.

A melanistic white-front was found with the Thames birds in January 1966 and with the Sheppey ones in February. A similar bird was seen in Belgium in 1965 and two in Cornwall in 1967, with further reports from Holland during this time.

It has long been accepted that the European white-front required

53. The picture shows the melanistic bird which joined the flock in 1966.

grazed pasture with shallow flashes of flood water for its wintering grounds. Indeed this was thought to be a limiting factor to its winter distribution.

For this reason, the change of farming from livestock grazing to cereals, both on the Thames and Sheppey, gave rise to concern for the future of this goose. There is little doubt that in North Kent flooded pastures are still the most favoured food source, but winter wheat is being grazed more extensively, a habit which may well have originated in the great goose reserve on the new Dutch polder of East Flevoland where winter wheat is now regularly grazed. From an agricultural viewpoint, this causes the wheat to 'tiller out' and is therefore beneficial, except in very wet weather. For the goose, the wheat has a higher protein value than winter grass and is therefore a better food, so there is no agricultural conflict here. According to D. J. Philippona, the polder white-fronts are now taking sixty to seventy per cent grass, twenty to thirty per cent winter wheat and ± ten per cent of other foods *(in litt.)*.

159

Greylag Goose

The history of the greylag in North Kent is most interesting. In the diaries of Richard Hayes (1725/90), there is an intriguing entry concerning the Thames marshes around Chalk, for on 12th July, 1774 he wrote, 'We found ye flapper season over. Geese too seem sometimes to have come inland.'

This strongly suggests to us that greylags, which were known to be breeding at that time at least as far south as Suffolk, were also breeding in North Kent and had by that time completed their moult on the estuary and were flying again into the marshes.

It is strange that there are no definite records of greylag in North Kent until 1937, when one was identified on Sheppey on 19th January. The next was shot on 5th January, 1939. Observations during the war years were almost impossible, but on 3rd January, 1947, about sixty were found among 500 white-fronts on the Thames, five being seen on Sheppey on 2nd March and the last on the Thames on 5th April.

Since 1953, greylags have become annual visitors to the North Kent Marshes as shown in the table.

Table 27: *Number of individual greylag geese 1953–74*

	1953	1954	1955	1956	1957	1958	1959	1960	1961	1962
Medway	1	—	1	2	—	4	—	26	12	—
Thames	4	3	1	7	30	4	18	4	14	2
Swale	—	—	5	14	—	4	1	4	8	2
Total	5	3	7	23	30	12	19	34	34	4

	1963	1964	1965	1966	1967	1968	1969	1970	1971	1972
Medway	1	2	1	—	—	5	9	—	—	—
Thames	6	2	1	2	7	1	21	—	—	—
Swale	2	3	2	—	—	17	46	20	23	52
Total	9	7	4	2	7	23	76	20	23	52

	1973	1974
Medway	—	—
Thames	61	60
Swale	40	30
Total	101	90

This gives an overall total of 585 birds considered to be migrants, of

Medway from the air. Milfordhope in the foreground; Greenborough and Burntwick ...ls beyond.

...on and waders on the reclaimed marsh of Barksore.

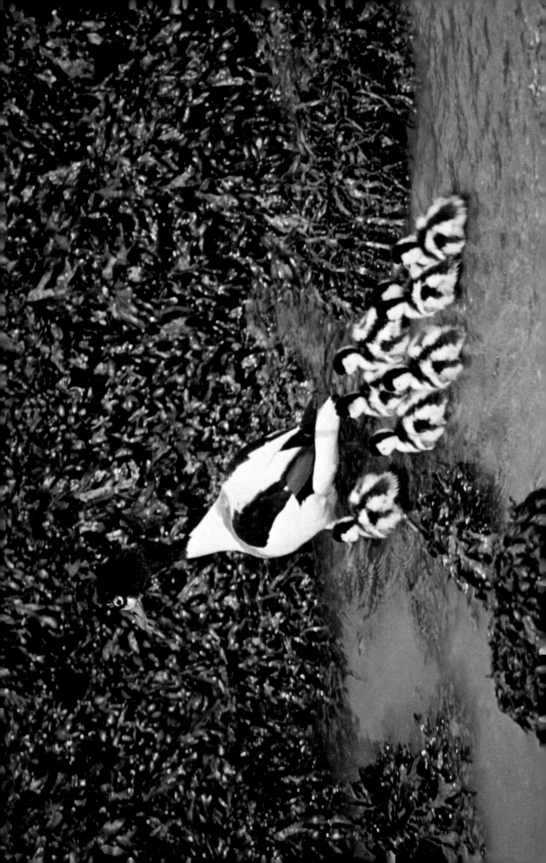

which 273 were from the Swale, 248 from the Thames and sixty-four from the Medway.

The monthly sightings show that the majority of these geese have been winter visitors:

Table 28: *Monthly sightings of greylag geese 1953–74*

Jan	Feb	Mar	Apr	May	Aug	Sept	Oct	Nov	Dec
203	129	60	10	2	2	2	54	76	161

The question now arises as to where these greylags originate, and there seems little doubt that many are immigrants from the European mainland – Scandinavian, Baltic and West Russian birds – many of which winter in the Low Countries or move through to the Iberian peninsula. This population shows intermediate characters between the typical orange-billed, dark-plumaged Icelandic/North British population and the pink-billed, pale-plumaged eastern greylag, which nests in Russia, east of the Urals and Lower Volga.

Greylags showing pink on their bills have been noted in Kent on various occasions since 1929 and in North Kent these included three in 1961, one in September 1968, sixteen in January 1969, twenty-one from November 1969 to January 1970 and forty in October 1973. As yet there are no ringing records to prove the origin of these birds, but on field characters of those well seen, there is no doubt. In further support, on 29th October, 1973, during a large scale waterfowl migration off the coast of East Kent, eighteen greylags were identified and another was seen coming in from out to sea on 9th November.

It is interesting to speculate as to which population the former breeding greylags in south-east England belonged. Sadly, we shall never be sure, but it would seem logical to believe that these birds were more closely linked to the continental mainland than to the north British birds. The breeding summer moult cycle of Belgian greylags is about a month ahead of Scottish birds and the timing of the Belgian birds would conform to Richard Hayes' observations in 1774.

Since 1955, a new factor has developed with the establishment by Count Léon Lippens of a most successful breeding population based at Le Zwin, Belgium, which now numbers over 700 birds and other colonies have been established in Holland, where several thousand are now moulting in summer.

54. Greylag geese beside the Medway, the result of a successful effort at reintroduction by WAGBI

In order to encourage further movements between North Kent and the European mainland, WAGBI has established a greylag reserve on 2,000 acres of private farmland on the southern side of the Medway and the first birds were released there from Scotland and East Anglia in July 1970. By 1971, there were twenty-four free-winged birds, but four nesting pairs were unsuccessful. The first brood of seven matured in 1972 and the autumn count increased to thirty-eight. In 1973 three pairs reared twelve goslings and the autumn peak reached fifty-three. Next year saw five broods totalling twenty-two and the autumn peak was sixty-three, while in 1975, when the exact number of broods could not be determined, the new peak was 106.

In the summer of 1973, a further twenty-nine greylags were brought over from Belgium and released on the Medway Reserve, in the hope that these would 'home' to the European mainland and be the start of a new winter 'flyway' into North Kent. So far, three of these have been recaptured in Belgium, one shot in Holland and two in Denmark, so they certainly 'homed', but it has been unfortunate that the recent winters have been so mild.

Meanwhile, the population is building up, looking magnificent, and the Kent Wildfowlers' Association has imposed a voluntary ban on greylag shooting since 1970. It now seems likely that this goose will flourish and may well eventually draw more continental birds over in winter.

Russian or Dark-breasted Brent Goose

Recent remarkable increases in the Russian Brent are a reflection of the general increase in the world total of this goose which reached a peak of about 100,000 in the winter of 1975/76, from a low of probably under 10,000 in the early 1950's.

In *Wildfowl in Great Britain*, the Brent counts were expressed as the average annual peak and the maximum count and these are set out for comparison for the Swale and Medway up to 1974/75.

Table 29: *Brent counts for the Medway and Swale 1953–75*

Winters	1953/54 to 1960/61	1961/62 to 1970/71	1971/72 to 1974/75
Medway			
Average annual peak	45	138	696
Maximum	105	400	766
Swale			
Average annual peak	110	346	732
Maximum	270	1040	1020

The past status of this goose is full of interest, but it is sad that there are no counts available prior to the 1930's, when a mycetozoan disease decimated the eel-grass (*Zostera*) beds, which provided its main food supply. One must remember that the need to count was not apparent in those days and we can only quote Norman Ticehurst who wrote in 1909 of immense flocks visiting the Thames, Medway and Swale in severe weather.

By the late 1930's, following the loss of the brent's staple diet, the story is very different. By now, up to fifty could be seen irregularly on the Thames, and, once in December 1938, a gaggle of 200, which was also seen briefly on the Medway in the same month. At this time there were very few other records from the Medway, but up to 250 could be seen on the Swale.

There were no observations during the war winters of 1939–45, but by 1946/47 a low point had been reached with peaks of only eighteen on the Swale, twenty on the Thames and thirteen on the Medway, where forty were reported next year and a hundred on the Swale in 1949. A skein of seventy-five seen by David Harrison on the Medway on 20th September, 1951, is the earliest record of a sizeable party. The recovery, therefore, has taken place during at least the past twenty-five years, with overall fluctuations according to breeding success.

Since 1954, the percentage of young in the flocks has ranged from virtually none to fifty-three per cent, with five years in that period with less than five per cent young in the flocks, in those years in which the breeding grounds are thought never to have unfrozen.

On the Thames, where small numbers began to be seen regularly in 1961, brent have occasionally numbered between 2–300 and they are being attracted to regenerating beds of *Zostera marina* which appeared on Roas Sand about five years ago.

The seasonal pattern shows two distinct features, an autumn peak, once in October, but otherwise in November, most often noted on the Swale, occasionally on the Medway or Thames, of only a few days' duration. These are presumed to be birds moving through to the south coast or France. This is followed by the wintering birds which now normally start to increase in late November to early December, moving south from Foulness and Leigh-on-Sea as the *Zostera* beds there are eaten out. A lone barnacle goose with the Essex brent in the winters of 1969/70 and 1970/71, was seen with brent on the Swale in early 1971.

Since the winter of 1972/73, no less than 817 Russian brent have been ringed and colour marked in Essex and East Anglia by what is now the Wildfowl Trust's pioneering brent goose research team headed by Andrew St Joseph. Sufficient marked brent have been sighted on the Medway and Swale to leave no doubt that our wintering birds move across from Essex and indeed there are a number of sightings of skeins moving across.

One individual ringed with the large Darvic ring at Foulness in December 1974, was identified on the Medway later that month, and was probably there until April 1975, when it re-appeared at Foulness, next being seen twelve days later in April on Texel in Holland and in May on the German Friesian Island of Föhr. Another ringed at Foulness in January 1973, was sighted at Seasalter next December, at Shoeburyness from October–December 1974, Harty Ferry in January 1975, back at Shoeburyness in February and on Föhr in April and May 1975.

An unexpected feature has come to light since regular sea watching started off East Kent in 1970. It now seems that there is a regular northward migration of brent off Thanet in October and November, which is presumed to be birds which have 'overshot' Essex and are working their way back, particularly as these movements are most marked during strong north-west winds. This might account in part for the short-lived autumn peaks on the Swale, but there is also a two-way passage at this time with other birds coasting towards the south coast.

In the autumn of 1975, an overland route from the Essex shore of the Thames Estuary to the English Channel was first noted. On 7th October, G. Graves saw thirty-one brent flying south over the Medway Estuary at 1,000 feet altitude. Then on 19th October, E. Still identified 140 more flying south-south-west over Headcorn on a direct overland route across Kent from the Essex coast. In all, a total of 1,030 brent were identified going south or south-west over Kent up to 11th November, after which no more were reported.

The peak movement was during the north-east gale of 8th–9th November when two skeins were seen flying south-west near Maidstone and others over Staplehurst, the Medway Estuary and the Swale, the two latter both heading inland. On those two wild days, there were 1,000 brent on both the Kentish Thames and the Swale and 550 on the Medway, to give the highest total ever known on the North Kent Marshes of 2,550.

On those two days a total of 910 headed west past Cliffe and did not reappear, a hundred being seen moving on past Tilbury on the 8th by J. Black. Soon after this brent 'upheaval' a complete albino was found among the remaining 400 on the Medway which remained until early spring.

Meanwhile one can only speculate as to this sudden spate of overland movements in the autumn of 1975. The overland route to Chichester Harbour would cut sixty miles off the flight by crossing Kent and rather more by flying west up the Thames and then south-west over Surrey and Hampshire, which is what appears to be happening. Presumably the route must have been explored in previous autumns by some pioneering brent, and it will be of great interest to see if it now becomes a regular route.

In North Kent, the main feeding grounds are on the south shore of the East Swale and on the southern side of the Medway Estuary. On the Swale, their main diet is eel-grass and on the Medway the greater part of their food is the green seaweeds (*Enteromorpha*), although eel-grass (*Zostera marina*) is increasing, particularly around Nor, which is now being increasingly used by brent. On big tides, the higher salting grasses are grazed both on the Swale and Medway. Occasional small parties of brent move round onto Stoke Saltings from Roas Bank on the flood tide.

Although in Essex brent are regularly moving to feed on inland pastures and winter wheat from mid-winter, this did not happen at all regularly in Kent, although occasional birds did so on Sheppey, and in March 1969 about eighty moved onto Barksore Farm for the high protein early bite. This happened again in December 1975 and from then on until their departure in spring up to 450 fed regularly on grass both on Barksore and Chetney, beside the Medway and 300 were doing the same on the Isle of Sheppey. On the Thames at Cooling up to forty regularly fed on winter wheat that same winter.

It is interesting to note that the increases in North Kent are not directly linked with breeding success, the then highest usage on the Medway occurring in the winter of 1974/75, when there were less than twenty young in England.

In the winters following the two good breeding years of 1972/73, some interesting observations at Leigh-on-Sea in comparison with the South Medway Estuary suggested that that part of the Medway was being used as a pairing-off area in late winter for second year birds, for there was an obvious separation of pairs with young, which remained on the eel-grass at Leigh and the second year birds which moved across to the South Medway to graze the lower protein green seaweeds, where they were often seen displaying.

Table 30 demonstrates these changes in age structure.

Table 30: *Age structure comparisons between Leigh-on-Sea and the South Medway 1972/73 and 1973/74*

| | Percentage Young | | |
	November Leigh	Feb–March Leigh	Jan–Feb South Medway
1972/73	41·6	74·3	2·4
1973/74	38·5	73·2	7·1

In the latter winter, it was interesting to note that those brent using the Swale consisted of 55·1 per cent young and on Roas Bank 43·7 per cent young and this was also approximately the age structure of those few which occasionally visited the North Medway.

In the winter of 1974/75, a winter in which no young were found in Kent, it was apparent that the same display was taking place among those brent on the South Medway, but the population was more erratic, possibly because the older brent elsewhere without young were more tolerant of second year birds.

In the winter of 1975/76, when a peak of 1,140 brent were using the Medway these changes in the population structure appeared to break down, although this was not complete. Thus on 31st December there were no young in a flock of eighty-seven on Milfordhope, but on 23rd January, a flock of 400 feeding on the freshmarsh grass on Barksore contained forty per cent young, in a year in which the total young exceeded fifty per cent. It seemed possible that the older brent with their young were partly keeping the second year birds out on the estuary away from the high protein grass.

As already mentioned, following the pollution of the Medway by oil from the *Seestern* in September 1966, attempts to clean the estuary with detergents decimated the green seaweeds over the whole southern part, and the brent decrease that winter was over eighty per cent compared with the average for the previous six years, due to an absence of food.

Light-breasted Brent Goose

This race of brent is uncommon in North Kent, the first being seen on the Swale on 9th October, 1945, and three more there on the late date of 14th May, 1946. Since then, fifteen were seen on Chetney on 17th March, 1956, eight at Allhallows on 14th December, 1957, two on the Swale on 1st February, 1960, and another, long dead, on Chetney on 3rd April, 1963. One was seen at Nor on 20th February, 1969, fifteen at Shellness on 29th December, 1971, and four others there on 24th December, 1973.

These birds could be either from Spitzbergen, North Greenland or Canadian Arctic breeding grounds. As yet we do not know which, but a Canadian bird ringed by Andrew St Joseph was recently reported from the Channel Islands.

167

Pacific Brent Goose

A fine example of this Far Eastern Siberian race of brent, with a complete white neck collar, black underparts and contrasting white flanks was well seen with the Russian brent on the South Medway in February 1974 and was the first record for Kent.

Shelduck

The shelduck is a characteristic bird of the North Kent Marshes, which regularly hold over two per cent of the north-west European population in midwinter, with peaks of over four per cent. The area is therefore in a very high category of international importance for this species.

Over the past decade, there has been a winter decrease, which applies particularly to the Thames and there is little doubt that a high proportion of these missing birds can be accounted for by those which have been found on the Inner Thames during the same period, for the total of the regular counts show that about 2,000 have been lost.

During the same period there has been a marked increase in those using the Medway Estuary, in common with other ducks. These changes are set out in the table.

Table 31: Regular and maximum counts of shelduck on the North Kent Marshes 1952–75

		1952–61	1961–66	1966–71	1971–75
Medway Estuary (S)	Regular	325	845	1391	1690
	Max	1000	3000	2500	2920
Medway Estuary (N)	Regular	—	—	443	300
	Max	100	250	950	520
Thames	Regular	4670	4200	1046	627
	Max	10,000	9000	1950	2000
Swale	Regular	785	779	845	823
	Max	3000	2500	5000	2000
Total of regular counts		5,780	5,824	3,725	3,440

All these figures represent a big increase during this century, for Prentis, writing in 1894, knew it only as a hard weather visitor to the Medway, while in 1909, Ticehurst wrote that he had seen flocks of 8–15 in North Kent in winter 'while Mr Hepburn states that on one occasion he had seen as many as 200 in a single flock.'

By 1950, Gillham and Homes were able to quote figures of 2–3,000 between Lower Hope and Egypt Bay and 1,000 off Allhallows, while the Medway normally held flocks of fifty, occasionally 2–300 on the southern shore and at Hoo. The Swale held an average winter population of 2–300, exceeded only in 1947 when 610 were counted at Elmley.

Peter Olney's food studies on the Medway showed that shelduck were feeding mainly on the intertidal zone mollusc *Hydrobia ulvae*, with smaller amounts of green seaweeds.

Such a limited diet obviously renders shelduck highly susceptible to severe weather and they duly suffered losses in the arctic winter of 1962/63, when the intertidal zone froze for up to sixteen days at a time. Of 106 shelduck found dead, fifty-one were sexed and forty-three were found to be females, indicating, as with wigeon, that males are more hardy than females.

It is possible that shelduck were forced to find new foods during

55. A pair of shelduck on their nesting territory on Chetney.

this spell and the move to the Inner Thames and also along the Medway inland of Rochester bridge could owe its origin to that cold spell.

It is interesting to note that following the Medway oil pollution by the *Seestern* and the massive destruction of shelduck foods by the cleansing operation, there was a much greater decrease in shelduck than in the severe weather, indicating the dangers to this species of a massive oil spill in the area. The recent dispersal of their main concentrations is therefore an excellent thing.

The breeding population is exceedingly difficult to assess, due to the fact that shelduck do not breed in their first, and probably not in their second year. Certainly the breeding population has increased greatly for Ticehurst wrote of only scattered pairs on the Swale and Thames, mentioning a concentration of thirty pairs on Cooling Marshes.

The Medway saltings and islands were surveyed by the Kent Ornithological Society at intervals since 1955 when the following nesting pairs were found:

Table 32: *Pairs of Shelduck on the Medway Estuary*

1955	1961	1966	1967	1972
18	25	66	42	74

The survey was repeated in 1967 following the *Seestern* oil pollution in 1966 to assess the resulting decreases.

The large increase in 1972 was largely accounted for by the greatly increased number of rabbit holes on Barksore seawall, where twenty-two pairs nested. The Chetney peninsula held thirty-two pairs in 1968/69.

The Swale was surveyed by the KOS for the four years 1961–64, with a peak of seventy-seven pairs in 1961 and a low of seventy-one pairs in 1964. No surveys have been made since.

On the Thames there would appear to have been a decline, for the same KOS survey from 1961–64 revealed a peak of sixty-five pairs in 1961 and a low of forty-seven pairs in 1964. In 1972, six broods were found at Cliffe and ten at Cooling, while thirteen pairs were thought to be nesting on the Isle of Grain in 1973, which could indicate about twenty-nine pairs along the Thames in 1972/73.

It has been suggested that the decline of the rabbit is responsible for the shelduck decline on the Thames, but rabbits are now back in good numbers, although so far no corresponding shelduck increase has been noted.

Between 4–500 non-breeding shelduck summer on the Thames and considerably fewer on the Medway and Swale. Shelduck leave the North Kent Marshes from mid-summer onwards, undertaking a moult migration to remote sandbanks in the Heligoland Bight, particularly the Grosse Knecksand.

Ringing recoveries have now proved the Heligoland/North Kent link and shelduck begin to return in numbers in November reaching a peak between December and February, depending upon the severity of the weather. Thereafter they disperse to their breeding grounds.

Wigeon

The wigeon is the commonest duck wintering on the North Kent Marshes, peak numbers usually occurring in January, but showing a wide variation and a marked increase, except in the astonishingly mild winter of 1974/75, when the expected January influx never occurred.

Table 33: *Annual peak counts of wigeon on the North Kent Marshes 1961–75*

Year	Count	Month	Year	Count	Month
1961/62	7,700	Dec	1968/69	19,740	Jan
1962/63	9,100	Feb	1969/70	14,600	Jan
1963/64	7,100	Jan	1970/71	15,600	Jan
1964/65	5,150	Dec	1971/72	13,000	Jan
1965/66	10,600	Jan	1972/73	10,780	Jan
1966/67	14,200	Jan	1973/74	13,080	Jan
1967/68	14,300	Jan	1974/75	7,780	Dec

Table 34: *Regular and maximum counts of wigeon 1952–75, demonstrating the massive increase on the Medway Estuary, very largely at the expense of the Thames.*

		1952–61	1961–66	1966–71	1971–75
Medway Estuary (S)	Regular	695	2,140	4,277	5,855
	Max	1,500	4,300	8,000	8,600
Medway Estuary (N)	Regular	150	311	622	556
	Max	200	1,000	1,100	1,000
Thames	Regular	3,825	2,318	2,766	1,100
	Max	15,000	5,000	10,640	2,000
Swale	Regular	1,230	1,887	3,757	2,050
	Max	5,000	5,000	6,000	3,400
Total of regular counts		5,900	6,656	11,422	9,561

There has certainly been an increase in this past half century, for in the 1930's, Gillham and Homes quote peak counts of 3–4,000 for the Thames and Swale and rather less for the Medway, prior to which there are no details.

Another notable feature has been the increasing number arriving on the Medway in September. In 1970, a record 1,500 was without precedent, but numbers in excess of 1,000 have occurred in four of the next five Septembers. This is the culmination of a trend which was first noted in 1966.

Wigeon foods were studied on the Medway between 1957–64. Until the onset of hard weather, most of the feeding is on the intertidal flats and the food was then found to consist almost entirely of green seaweeds, together with seeds of marsh samphire and orache. However, in October 1970, by which time eel-grass was re-establishing itself well, no less than eight out of twelve wigeon examined were taking this food, which has a higher protein content than the green seaweeds.

From mid-winter, wigeon start regular flighting to the brackish marshes to feed on various grasses and the leaves of fennel-leaved pondweed in the ditches and fleets. In early spring, they move to the high protein 'early bite' of the richer pastures.

The timing of the move away from the intertidal zone depends upon the availability of the food there, on the onset of hard weather and especially on the presence of any flooding of the grazing marshes, which makes them much more attractive. In recent years, winter wheat has also attracted wigeon at this time of year so that wigeon tend to move from the Medway to both the Thames and Swale. If the freshmarshes become hard frozen, wigeon re-concentrate on the Medway. However, in very mild winters, wigeon continue to find adequate food on the mudflats throughout the whole winter and very little flighting occurs.

A detailed study of daily or weekly fluctuations clearly demonstrate that wigeon using the Swale are composed of a large proportion of birds which are moving through, whereas those on the Medway are more sedentary, so that the 'holding capacity' of the Medway is considerably higher than the Swale.

In mild winters, wigeon will return early to the European mainland. On 6th and 7th February, 1972, a total of at least 1,000 were seen to leave the Medway in several flocks in the late afternoon, flying high to the north-east towards Holland.

A remarkable fact has recently been revealed about the population structure of the North Kent wigeon flocks by WAGBI's duck wing

56. Wigeon overhead.

surveys, for a marked preponderance of adult drakes has been found in the samples ranging from 229 adult drakes in 1972/73 to 249 in 1973/74 per every hundred adult females, whereas no such difference is found in the young birds.

As yet, the whereabouts of the 'missing' adult females is unknown, as is the reason for this marked differential migration. It is probable that the females may migrate further to the south-west for severe winters exert more of an adverse effect on duck than drake wigeon in Kent. In the hard weather of 1947, the wigeon flocks on the Medway split up, the ducks coming in to feed in the lee of sea walls, whereas the drakes were strong enough to stay out on the more exposed saltings.

In the very severe winter of 1962/63, this went further and there was both a differential emigration of ducks away from the cold and a differential mortality rate. Of the sexed casualties from exposure, fifty-six per cent were ducks at a time when the remaining flocks were made up of seventy-five per cent drakes.

173

There are only six nesting records – the first four all on Sheppey – a nest found by a shepherd in 1915; a pair with young found by John Wacher in 1918; a nest with eggs found by Arnold Churchill in 1932 and a duck with eight young seen by Tom Gregory in 1956. In 1971 JGH saw two pairs on Chetney through the summer and in late July, one had young just able to fly and the second pair was also found with flying young two weeks later. Other pairs have summered in 1948, 1950, 1959, 1961, 1962 and 1974. Solitary drakes have been seen more often and it could be that

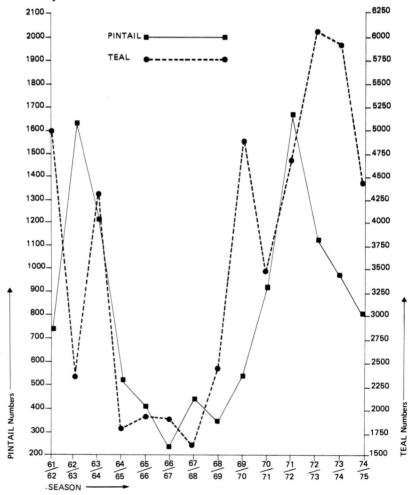

Figure 7. Annual peak numbers of teal and pintail on the North Kent Marshes 1961–62 to 1974–75.

wigeon are slowly extending their breeding range southwards, as all these records, except the first three, are from the past twenty years.

Gadwall

In 1909, Ticehurst in his *Birds of Kent* could only record three gadwall, a pair taken in Grovehurst Decoy and a duck shot in 1860. On 3rd June, 1922 a duck on Faversham marshes was behaving as if with young. Another was shot on Blythe Sands in February 1927 and the next was seen in the winter of 1936/37. The following winter two immatures and a pair were seen on the Thames marshes. Two others were seen there in the following winter and a pair on 17th March, 1940.

In 1946, a pair was seen on the Thames in the spring and on 29th August, JGH found a pair with flying young. Gillham and Homes found a pair with small young in the same spot next June. In 1948, two pairs were present in spring, but it was a drought summer and no breeding took place. Five or six were seen next winter and breeding was probably attempted in 1949. One pair was seen there in 1951, an eclipse drake shot on 12th August, 1951 and on 1st December James Harrison saw a duck on Barksore, the first record for the Medway.

Since then the increases can be tabulated.

Table 35: *Number of pairs of gadwall with peak autumn/winter counts in brackets*

	1952	1953	1954	1955	1956	1957	1958	1959
Medway	—	—	1	—	—	(3)	—	(2)
Thames	1 (2)	— (2)	1 (3)	— (2)	1 (4)	— (3)	— (3)	1 (3)
Swale	—	—	—	(3)	—	1 (4)	— (3)	— (3) — (4)

	1960	1961	1962	1963	1964	1964	1966	1967
Medway	— (3)	— (3)	— (5)	— (2)	1 (3)	—	— (2)	— (3)
Thames	1 (9)	1 (5)	2 (3)	— (4)	— (3)	— (3)	— (5)	2(22)
Swale	— (3)	2 (8)	1 (4)	1 (3)	1 (2)	1 (2)	1 (8)	— (2)

	1968	1969	1970	1971	1972	1973	1974
Medway	— (5)	— (5)	1 (8)	1 (5)	2 (4)	—(10)	—(10)
Thames	2(22)	2(28)	1(32)	1(38)	—(40)	7(24)	2(17)
Swale	— (2)	1 (3)	1 (5)	1 (4)	— (6)	— (6)	—(10)

During this period at least six breeding pairs have been found on the Medway, twenty-five on the Thames and eleven on the Swale, almost half in the last eight years, so that the gadwall is slowly increasing as a breeding bird and as a winter visitor, when the majority are found on the Thames at Cliffe Pools. These birds could have originated in East Anglia where the population has increased, or in West Kent where hand-reared birds have been liberated by WAGBI. Others are undoubtedly immigrants from north-west Europe and an observation of six flying west into the Thames off Allhallows on 22nd September, 1973 and two others a week later is of interest.

Teal

The Medway is now the most important estuary for teal in Britain, lying as it does in the main migrational flyway for those moving south-west from Holland. The Medway has become steadily of greater importance since detailed counting first started in 1952, the increase being at the expense of both the Thames and Swale, although a true and substantial increase has occurred as shown by the total of regular counts.

Table 36: *Regular and Maximum teal figures for the four main areas 1952–75*

		1952–61	1961–66	1966–71	1971–75
Medway Estuary (S)	Regular	535	1289	1610	3245
	Max	2000	2180	4050	5365
Medway Estuary (N)	Regular	—	93	520	473
	Max	100	300	1480	2000
Thames	Regular	1860	624	199	363
	Max	3600	1500	320	1000
Swale	Regular	600	653	335	332
	Max	3000	3000	750	545
Total of regular counts		2995	2659	2664	4413

This method of showing teal population changes in fact obscures the years of the great decline between the winters of 1964/65 and 1968/69. These are shown graphically and are surprisingly similar to pintail changes, although this was not appreciated at the time. (Fig. 7, p 174.)

The teal decline was noted from most parts of Britain and gave rise to considerable concern. There could only be two possible explanations; the first that it was a true decline, associated with poor breeding success and/or excessive mortality; second that there had

Bewick's swans – now regular visitors to the North Kent Marshes.

Russian Brent geese feeding on *Zostera* off Leigh-on-Sea.

Flying inland to feed on grass in South Essex.

been a migratory shift, taking teal elsewhere. No such decline was noted for instance in the massive Camargue population in France.

Another factor which must be remembered is that in 1961/62 the population was still at a high level following the massive displacement of teal when the new Dutch polder of East Flevoland was drained in 1959. The most recent peak is also probably the resulting displacement from South Flevoland, the latest polder to be drained. It is still very difficult therefore to assess the 'normal' wintering teal population on the North Kent Marshes.

The problem of the mid-1960's decline provided the first practical test for WAGBI's Duck Production Surveys, which started in the winter of 1965/66 and from then on, 250–350 wings from shot teal had been sexed and aged annually from Kent, with the following results.

Table 37: *Percentage of young teal in the shooting bag 1965–71*

Season	1965/66	1966/67	1967/68	1968/69	1969/70	1970/71
Percentage young	63·9	67·1	68·1	56·1	62·1	65·5

Assuming a similar annual bias in the shooting bag, it is apparent that the first three seasons, which included the lowest level to which the national population index fell (1967/68), as monitored by the

57. A pack of teal. The Medway is the most important estuary in Britain for this species.

Wildfowl Trust, included the three best breeding seasons, assessed from wing analysis. In the winter of 1968/69, the first signs of increase were detected and this was well confirmed in the next winter and this in spite of two comparatively poor breeding seasons. This seemed to be strong evidence in favour of a migratory shift.

Considered with hindsight, some kind of cyclical rhythm seems to be appearing in both teal and pintail, which is extremely interesting. Prior to 1951, before the National Wildfowl counts were fully established, there were few counts to justify any conclusions about the earlier status of teal in North Kent. A count of 2,000 on the Thames in December 1946 during a hard spell, is referred to by Gillham and Homes as exceptional, so there can be little doubt that a marked increase has occurred.

The feeding habits of teal on the Medway salt and brackish marshes were studied by Peter Olney, who found their main foods to be the mollusc *Hydrobia ulvae* and seeds of marsh samphire, seablite and orache on saltmarsh, and seeds of sea club rush and fennel-leaved pondweed on brackish marshes.

Marsh samphire is the most favoured food and on 24th December, 1969, in the best seeding year we have ever known, there were 4,000 teal feeding on twenty acres of flooded marsh samphire on Chetney Marsh.

Teal breed in scattered pairs in the North Kent Marshes, but not annually until 1959, since when only in 1971 were no pairs located in the breeding season. In this period, thirty-three pairs have been found on the Swale marshes, twenty-seven on the Thames and eighteen on the Medway. All of the latter have been recorded only since 1966 and fifteen of these since 1969.

This was the year in which WAGBI carried out an interesting experiment, following some breeding experiments first carried out at Netherby on the Solway at the end of the nineteenth century.

Briefly, twenty-one teal caught in WAGBI's Boarstall decoy were kept in a special aviary on the south side of the Medway. In early March, they were ringed and released on Barksore at the same time having their primaries pulled from one wing. It took five weeks for the new feathers to grow, the idea being that by rendering them flightless for the time of spring migration, they would settle down and breed in the release area and that their young would return to nest in the area where they were hatched.

This certainly appeared to have worked, for four broods were found that year in the release area and two other pairs on the north shore may well have bred.

Next year, nine more teal were released in this way; two more broods were found nearby and a further pair located on the north shore. No further releases have yet been made, but the fact that fifteen breeding pairs have been located on the estuary since 1969 is certainly rather encouraging.

Mallard

The mallard is a common nesting species, its numbers being augmented by immigrants from the continent in winter. There are thus two peaks, an early autumn one when the home-bred birds have flocked and a winter one which varies in time according to weather conditions. There is usually a marked drop in numbers in October, but as so few home-bred mallard are being ringed, there is no evidence as to where these birds go.

Table 38: *Regular and maximum mallard figures for the four main areas 1952–75*

		1952/61	1961–66	1966–71	1971–75
Medway Estuary (S)	Regular	100	459	981	856
	Max	230	1200	2000	2000
Medway Estuary (N)	Regular	50	94	500	806
	Max	120	200	900	2600
Thames	Regular	1840	1385	569	822
	Max	2900	2000	1050	2000
Swale	Regular	970	762	819	1110
	Max	2000	2000	2000	2080
Total of regular counts		2960	2700	2869	3594

Over this period the Medway Estuary has steadily increased in importance and until 1971 the Thames was declining whereas the Swale had remained almost unchanged. In the past four years, however, both Thames and Swale have shown an increase and the overall total of regular counts now shows a definite increase.

The last complete nesting census was organised by the Kent Ornithological Society in 1963 when a total of 401 pairs was found as follows: Medway Estuary and freshmarshes 150, Thames 103 and Swale 148. The Swale was fully covered again in the next two years, 140 pairs being found each year. Increases on the Medway

Estuary have been established by the five K OS censuses when the following pairs were found:

Table 39: *Pairs of Mallard on the Medway Estuary*

1955	1961	1966	1967	1972
37	69	53	94	91

In 1968/69, we calculated that the Medway and its surrounding freshmarshes held a total of 270 pairs, including eighty-four pairs on Chetney, thirty pairs at Kingsnorth, twenty-five pairs on Barksore, twelve pairs at Motney Hill and twenty-five pairs along Stoke and Yantlet fleets.

An exciting mid-summer moulting area developed on the Medway following the reclamation of Barksore by the Moulands in 1965. The tidal creeks became lagoons sheltered with a dense growth of hastate orache and by 1970 this cover was being used by a large population of moulting mallard. The eastern reed-fringed lagoon at Kingsnorth was also used as a pre-moult assembly ground. By late June there were 410 adult drake and 125 adult duck mallard at Kingsnorth and Barksore combined, but by mid-July at least 500 adult mallard were concentrated on Barksore, Kingsnorth being virtually deserted.

If one assumes a static nesting population on the Swale of 140 pairs and 270 pairs on the Medway, then the Barksore total of 410 drakes corresponds exactly, and from this we deduced that Barksore was being used as a moulting area for most of the Medway and Swale mallard.

For the past two summers, however, a large part of Barksore has been seeded with grass and grazed by sheep, so that nesting and moulting cover is no longer available. In the autumn of 1974, some 2,000 mallard from the Thames were using the Kingsnorth east lagoon and reed beds as a day roost, flighting across the Hoo peninsula, but by 1975, this too was flooded with the change to coal burning at the power station and the Thames mallard have reverted to their more usual autumn roosts on Cliffe Fleet and the open Thames, while the reed-fringed fleets are again being utilised for moulting.

It is highly likely that the release of hand-reared mallard in North Kent by the Kent W A has been an important factor in the build-up of the population and these W AGBI-ringed birds may provide a clue to

58. Mallard flighting to stubble on the Thames study area.

the decreasing numbers in October, for there are now a number of recoveries in both France and Holland.

Pintail

The pintail is an increasingly common winter visitor, but with a cycle of abundance and scarcity and showing a major shift away from the Thames and Swale to the Medway Estuary. The table sets out this trend.

The cyclical change is best shown graphically based on annual peak numbers on the North Kent Marshes and as already mentioned, there is a similarity with the teal situation. This time, however, the draining of new Dutch polders cannot be considered a factor, as the main pintail concentrations are further south, in the Scheldt (Fig. 7, p. 174).

181

Table 40: *Regular and maximum counts of pintail 1952–75*

		1952–61	1961–66	1966–71	1971–75
Medway Estuary (S)	Regular	25	147	265	541
	Max	95	300	650	950
Medway Estuary (N)	Regular	—	—	167	246
	Max	—	—	434	650
Thames	Regular	230	546	71	155
	Max	800	1400	250	400
Swale	Regular	70	64	31	25
	Max	210	200	80	47
Total of regular counts		325	757	534	967

It is interesting to note how the pintail must have increased, for when Norman Ticehurst wrote his *Birds of Kent* in 1909, flocks of thirty were noteworthy. James Harrison, in his *Birds of Kent*, records that by 1951 these had been eclipsed by flocks of 300.

Within the Medway, which is now by far the most important area for pintail, the most remarkable feature has been the colonisation of the north shore, where until the winter of 1967/68, this duck was seldom seen. In January 1972, the peak count was 650, all close to Kingsnorth power station which was constructed in the 1960's. The pintail come here to roost at high tide on the two settling lagoons and in the lee of Oakham Island, which provides better shelter now that the oiling jetty has been constructed across it to the tanker terminal off Oakham Ness. On one big spring tide that month, what was thought to be the whole Medway population of 1,250 was found here.

It is interesting that this is a new population on the Medway, for those on the south shore around Greenborough are also increasing. Those using the Kingsnorth roost feed mainly on Nor Island.

It is not known why pintail are now favouring the Medway Estuary so much more in winter, but food must be a big factor. Peter Olney's studies on the Medway showed that they were taking very substantial amounts of the small marine mollusc *Hydrobia ulvae* and these were in fact present in every pintail examined. The pintail is therefore very susceptible to changes in the population of this mollusc, which is flourishing on the Medway. This cannot, however, explain the pintail's decline in the middle 1960's.

The decline on the Thames marshes could also be partly explained by the move westwards to the Inner Thames, but it was encouraging to note a recovery in the very wet winter of 1974/75, when the regular population was 253 and the maximum 400. An interesting count of 268 pintail seen flying west past Allhallows on 29th September, 1973 by Trevor Bowley and Lawrence Woollard, must have been part of the Inner Thames population arriving.

The first successful nesting of pintail was on the Thames in 1947, where Eric Gillham found a pair with young. Since then fifty-seven pairs are thought to have nested, many successfully, and where the localities have been reported, twenty-seven are from the Thames, nineteen from the Swale and five from the Medway.

Garganey

This is the only duck which is a summer visitor, extreme dates ranging from 27th February to 22nd October. Its preference is for brackish and freshmarshes, with well-sheltered reed-fringed lagoons in the fleets. Nests are sited in tall grass, nettles and growing corn. Two nests have been found on the saltings, on Sheppey in 1936 and on the Thames in 1946.

Passage migrants move through in spring and in wet springs more tend to remain to breed. The first nesting was not proved until 1933 when two nests were found, followed by two more in 1938 and 1942. Eric Gillham has recorded fourteen to fifteen pairs nesting along the Thames between 1946–48, and that the seven years 1945–52 were the golden years for this species with a total of close on thirty-five pairs nesting on the North Kent Marshes.

The following table sets out what is known since then of the number of pairs in each area, together with the peak counts in late

Table 41: *Summering pairs and peak autumn counts (in brackets) of garganey 1953–75*

	1953	1954	1955	1956	1957	1958	1959	1960
Medway	?	?	?	Extremely	Extremely	Eight	?(11)	—(25)
Thames	V. few	1	A few	low	low	pairs	6(40)	10(15)
Swale	6	?	?			in all	9(20)	7(40)

	1961	1962	1963	1964	1965	1966	1967	1968
Medway	1(6)	—	1(5)	—	—(4)	—(3)	—(5)	1(25)
Thames	4–5(31)	4	4–5(30)	8–9(48)	12–14(11)	?(14)	10(20)	?
Swale	11(30)	9(11)	11(53)	9(30)	?(30)	1(35)	3(40)	?

	1969	1970	1971	1972	1973	1974	1975
Medway	3(25)	—(10)	2(39)	3(14)	—	1	3(11)
Thames	4–5	2	2–4(12)	?(44)	5–6(6)	4(10)	4(20)
Swale	?	1(3)	—	—	—	1	?(1)

summer. It also shows extensive gaps in our knowledge which is perhaps inevitable with such a difficult species to study.

The interpretation of the table is difficult. Certainly 1953 saw a big decrease, possibly following the January surge tide which inundated virtually the whole nesting area, in which case why was the Swale so good? More recently, a real decline seems certain, which in the past five years at least may be related to drought conditions on the West African wintering grounds, where massive mortality has been recorded.

Similarly the autumn flocks are difficult to interpret, for garganey can often be overlooked among early packs of teal. Furthermore they are not necessarily indicative of breeding success, for inland observations have shown that passage migrants are moving through Kent from mid-June.

Shoveler

There are two populations of shoveler, home-bred birds and winter immigrants from north-west Europe. Peak counts are usually in August and March, when there is a marked passage migration which probably includes both groups. In wet springs, there is evidence suggesting that more stay to breed rather than continue to the Low Countries.

Table 42: *Regular and maximum counts of shoveler 1952–75*

		1952/61	1961–66	1966–71	1971–75
Medway Estuary (S)	Regular	—	23	140	117
	Max	150	50	300	300
Medway Estuary (N)	Regular	—	42	68	78
	Max	120	100	120	225
Thames	Regular	205	167	190	144
	Max	650	500	500	300
Swale	Regular	85	120	133	301
	Max	485	250	600	490
Total of regular counts		290	352	531	640

The totals of the regular counts show a steady rise and have more than doubled in this twenty-four-year period. On these figures all three areas now hold up to one per cent of the North-West European regional population, and are thus of international importance for shoveler.

In the winter of 1971/72, some remarkable counts were reported by B. Hawkes in the North Sea off the Isle of Sheppey with peaks of 2,400 in November, 3,100 in December, 1,050 in January and 1,200 in February. These concentrations were not found within our area, where the combined peak totals were 620 in December and 654 in January. Where these birds were feeding is quite unknown and one is almost left wondering if they could have been feeding at sea, which would be no less remarkable.

In 1950, E. Gillham and R. C. Homes estimated a breeding population of fifty to eighty pairs on the Cliffe-Hoo peninsula, the majority along the Thames, rather than the northern Medway. A smaller number were equally well established on Sheppey, indicating a total of about a hundred pairs. This figure was confirmed in the Kent Ornithological Survey in 1961–64.

The Medway until then was always considered unattractive for nesting shoveler due to lack of suitable brackish marshes other than Chetney and none has ever been found nesting on the Medway islands. However, in 1961, Harry Mouland found eight nests on Chetney and in 1968–71, JGH found seventeen, eighteen, twenty-four and twenty-seven pairs present respectively. Following the

59. A pair of shoveler; a frequent nester on the North Kent Marshes.

drainage at the northern end of the peninsula of about ten acres of shallows, which were their main attraction, only one pair nested in 1973, but in the very wet spring of 1975, W. F. A. Buck estimated that twenty pairs were nesting.

In North Kent, shoveler take up territories along the fleets and ditches of the fresh marshes, their nests being hidden in coarse grass or nettles. In 1975, in the 300-acre Thames study area of growing wheat, twelve pairs were nesting, having taken up territories beside pools of standing flood water in the crops. That spring there were thirty to thirty-five pairs along the Thames. Only occasionally do shoveler nest on saltings, usually beside the Swale.

It seems reasonable to assume that the North Kent Marshes can hold up to a hundred nesting pairs in good years. In 1971, B. Yarker and G. Atkinson-Willes estimated the British nesting population at 'certainly less than 1,000 pairs and probably less than 500'. Thus our area can hold ten to twenty per cent of this population.

Pochard

In 1909, Ticehurst referred to pochard as hard-weather visitors, much disturbed by shipping in the Thames, while Prentis in 1894 knew of only brief visits to the Medway. Indeed, until 1935 it remained a scarce winter visitor to the Thames with a maximum of a mere twenty-five. With the flooding of the first large clay pit at Cliffe in that year, there was an annual increase to a peak of 105 in January 1939.

In the severe winter of 1947, what was then a remarkable flock of 700 moved onto the Thames off Higham, while until 1960 pochard were seldom seen on either the Medway or Swale.

Table 43: *Regular and maximum counts of pochard 1952–75*

		1952–61	1961–66	1966–71	1971–75
Medway Estuary (S)	Regular	—	15	25	17
	Max	—	40	63	50
Medway Estuary (N)	Regular	—	112	115	94
	Max	150	360	150	166
Thames	Regular	185	339	333	417
	Max	610	950	600	732
Swale	Regular	20	78	60	99
	Max	100	250	200	220
Total of regular counts		205	544	533	627

Since 1952, wintering pochard have shown a steady increase, being attracted mainly to Cliffe Pools, Captain's Pool and the Kingsnorth lagoons, but with the changes now taking place on two of these sites, wintering pochard seem likely to decrease again. Peak numbers were recorded in the arctic winter of 1962–63.

Breeding was first recorded on the Thames in 1907 by three pairs, as in 1909. Single pairs bred there in 1937, 1938 and 1946. In 1947, three broods were found. Two pairs were present in 1948; one pair nested in 1950 and probably five pairs in 1951.

Since then, it is possible to tabulate the minimum number of nesting pairs in each area, but it must be remembered that the best observer cover was undoubtedly from 1961–65, during the Kent Ornithological Society's survey of breeding wildfowl.

Table 44: *The minimum number of pairs of breeding pochard 1952–74*

	1952	1953	1954	1955	1956	1957	1958	1959	1960
Medway	—	—	—	—	—	—	—	—	Approx.
Thames	2	11	8	14	20	18	18	17	Total
Swale	—	—	—	—	1	6	2	2	50
Total	2	11	8	14	21	24	20	19	50

	1961	1962	1963	1964	1965	1966	1967	1968	1969
Medway	6	3	3	2	1	increasing	3	4	6
Thames	17	20	30	20	23		12	10	10
Swale	16	22	21	24	16		7	?	6
Total	39	45	54	46	40		22	?	22

	1970	1971	1972	1973	1974
Medway	11	9	8	3	5
Thames	?	1	11	?	15
Swale	6	?	11	?	6
Total	?	?	30	?	26

It is apparent that the Thames was colonised from 1946, the Swale from 1956 and the Medway from 1961. The pochard requires stretches of open water to act as nursery grounds which have been provided by open areas in the bigger fleets on the Thames and Sheppey, a large lagoon on Chetney known as the 'Teal Hole' and on Murston clay pits since 1966. Pochard have also utilised the 'borrow dyke' along the inside of the Thames sea wall.

In 1971, Yarker and Atkinson-Willes estimated the British nesting population at only 200 pairs, confirming Parslow's original estimate in 1967. In that case, then the North Kent Marshes are extremely important nationally, holding ten to fifteen per cent of the British breeding stock on recent counts, perhaps more.

Tufted Duck

Ticehurst in 1909 looked upon the tufted as a hard weather migrant to the North Kent Marshes and it was still unusual on the Swale until 1950 and the Medway until 1960, although thirty-two were seen there in hard weather in January 1947.

Cliffe Pools provided the first attraction from 1936, when tufted duck became regular, 105 appearing in severe weather in January 1939 and 200 in February 1947. Steady increases there culminated in a massive 1,300 in the arctic winter of 1962/63, many of which were frozen off Cliffe Pools onto the open river. Decreases in 1966–71 could be accounted for by the colonisation of the Inner Thames. During this period, the Kingsnorth lagoons and Captain's Pool on the North Medway were also colonised. Now, with both Cliffe Pools and Kingsnorth lagoons being back-filled, a big decrease seems inevitable. These changes are set out in the table.

Table 45: *Regular and maximum counts of tufted duck 1952–75*

		1952–61	1961–66	1966–71	1971–75
Medway Estuary (S)	Regular	—	—	—	—
	Max	—	64	12	40
Medway Estuary (N)	Regular	—	—	77	44
	Max	—	74	109	68
Thames	Regular	165	430	375	319
	Max	550	1300	550	350
Swale	Regular	5	—	9	—
	Max	10	58	30	30
Total of regular counts		170	430	461	363

Winter migrants build up from October and whereas they formerly showed a January peak, this is no longer so marked and in two out of the past four years there have been November peaks, presumably of passage migrants. Most have left by the end of March.

The first breeding took place as recently as 1962, a brood being seen on Sheppey. Nests are in the proximity of the larger marshland fleets or in reed cover beside the various lagoons.

From 1962–74, thirty-one pairs have been found in territories by the Swale, nine pairs by the Thames and seventeen pairs by the Medway, totalling fifty-seven, and twenty-seven broods were seen.

Scaup

Up to 1950, the Scaup was an annual winter visitor in parties of six to eight birds. Since then there has been a definite increase, particularly in hard weather, which has been most striking since 1954, as shown in the table.

Increases on the Thames have been particularly impressive, attracted by Cliffe Pools. In the last five years, Kingsnorth lagoons have also become attractive.

Increases in North Kent must be related to increases in Holland, particularly on the Ijsselmeer. The only ringing recovery, however,

60. Scaup and a single tufted duck. In hard weather the former are the more numerous in North Kent.

Table 46: *Annual peak number of scaup 1939–74*

	1939*	1940*	1947*	1952	1953	1954*	1955	1956*
Medway	—	—	13	—	—	—	2	34
Thames	52	15	50	20	36	250	50	550
Swale	50	63	21	—	2	300	2	11

	1957	1958	1959	1960	1961	1962	1963*	1964
Medway	—	—	—	—	2	2	80	—
Thames	50	60	30	57	75	120	700	6
Swale	—	—	—	—	33	5	300	6

	1965	1966	1967	1968	1969	1970	1971	1972
Medway	2	6	2	4	50	25	20	4
Thames	20	8	7	25	7	18	10	10
Swale	—	4	1	16	20	3	27	4

	1973	1974
Medway	15	22
Thames	32	6
Swale	8	2

* Hard weather

is a drake ringed on Lake Myvatn, Iceland in May 1939 and recovered at Whitstable in the following February.

The earliest arrivals are occasionally seen in September, two on the Medway on 3rd September, 1967 being the earliest. In 1956, 150 were still present at Cliffe on 25th March, fifteen on 15th April and the last two on 5th June. In 1971, three were seen at St Mary's Bay on 22nd July.

Eider

It is only since 1952 that eiders have been regular in North Kent. Prior to this, three immatures were shot on the Medway between 1867–1894 and on the Swale eight were seen on 17th May, 1937; one was found dead in January 1938, three pairs were seen on 15th January, 1939 and six in December 1945.

What was probably a south-westward extension of range from Holland reached its peak in 1961–66 and is now declining again. The first British recovery of an overseas eider was a young bird from East Vlieland, one of the Dutch Friesian islands, ringed in July 1974 and recovered on the Swale next December.

61. Eider have become regular visitors, especially to the Swale.

The table shows the trend, with the Swale clearly the most favoured area, all being found at the eastern end.

Table 47: *Regular and maximum counts of eider 1952–75*

		1952–61	1961–66	1966–71	1971–75
Medway	Regular	—	22	—	—
	Max	25	60	8	35
Thames	Regular	—	12	—	—
	Max	27	40	50	40
Swale	Regular	10	43	44	22
	Max	40	206	80	50
Total of regular counts		10	77	44	22

Although peak numbers in general occur in mid-winter, fifty were seen on the Swale in April and October 1972. Although there are only under twenty per cent of adult drakes reported, adults of both sexes are now frequent enough in the summer to make breeding a distinct possibility. A definite increase in July in the peak years of 1961–66 gave rise to hopes that a moult migration was becoming established to the eastern Swale, but this has stopped.

Common Scoter

The common scoter, although a truly marine duck in winter, is a regular visitor to the eastern Swale and the Thames Estuary, but is much less regular in the land-locked Medway Estuary. Writing in 1950, Gillham and Homes were twice able to record flocks of 2–300 off Cliffe, in November 1934 and 1936. The most they knew of in the Swale was only twenty to thirty.

The comparative figures over the past twenty-four years show a major increase during the decade 1952–61 with the Swale becoming the most important area, a decline in peak numbers but an increase in regular numbers during the next decade and an overall decrease during the past four years. The reason for the apparent switch from the Thames to the Swale is unknown.

Table 48: *Regular and maximum counts of common scoter 1952–61*

		1952–61	1961–66	1966–71	1971–75
Medway	Regular	—	10	—	—
	Max	20	30	20	80
Thames	Regular	75	137	73	20
	Max	1200	474	150	63
Swale	Regular	145	242	307	187
	Max	1500	1200	750	400
Total of regular counts		220	389	380	207

The majority of records fall between July–December, with November the peak month in seven out of the past fourteen years and October in four. However, common scoters have now been recorded in every month of the year, including flocks of fifty on the Swale in June, 350 in July and 500 in August. There is no marked spring migration, 130 on the Swale in March 1974 being the peak count.

Common scoters are most difficult to study and at present we know little about those in North Kent, although in November 1956, C. Wheeler noted that a flock of 350 in the Thames was made up entirely of juveniles. Finally, 600 were seen off Cliffe during a north-easterly gale on 9th November, 1975.

Goldeneye

Writing at the end of the nineteenth century, Walter Prentis stated that the largest party known on the Medway was seven, while Ticehurst in 1909 referred to similar numbers on the Swale and Thames.

By 1950, Gillham and Homes were able to record the first increases with up to ten on Cliffe pools in the winters of 1937/38 and 1938/39. A remarkably early record was of nearly fifty seen by R. G. Williams on the Swale on 24th September, 1939. In January 1946, JGH found forty on the Medway (East Hoo Creek) including ten adult drakes. There were twenty-four there next year, when Gillham also found twenty on the Thames including eight adult drakes.

Goldeneye are not easy to count. They move around over wide areas in small parties and on the Medway a boat is invaluable. For this reason, annual peak counts are probably more meaningful than data based on monthly counts. These peak counts occur in January or February. The averages show no significant changes during this period.

Table 49: *Peak counts and averages of goldeneye 1952–59, 1960–67 and 1968–74*

	1952	1953	1954	1955	1956	1957	1958	1959	Average
Medway	40	35	25	33	150	45	58	83	58·6
Thames	12	3	25	3	6	3	1	4	7·1
Swale	4	3	25	15	20	3	1	4	9·3

	1960	1961	1962	1963	1964	1965	1966	1967	Average
Medway	42	60	15	131	70	32	56	50	57·0
Thames	6	6	—	10	3	3	6	10	5·5
Swale	6	4	6	10	15	3	2	3	6·1

	1968	1969	1970	1971	1972	1973	1974		Average
Medway	30	32	48	100	50	50	107		59·6
Thames	10	12	10	15	19	14	17		13·8
Swale	5	1	4	8	16	20	7		8·7

The big channels of the Medway with their mussel beds are now the main goldeneye haunts in Kent, particularly Stangate, Halstow, Half Acre and East Hoo Creeks, birds normally being present from mid-October to late April, of which about twenty per cent are adult

193

drakes. Extreme dates are a drake at Windmill Creek on 8th August, 1961 and another at Cliffe on 17th May, 1974.

Red-breasted Merganser

The peak years for this 'saw-bill' were during the decade 1952–61, but the decline since then may have halted with some redistribution, the Swale and Thames showing marked decreases and the south Medway a slight increase. These results are tabulated below.

Table 50: *Regular and maximum counts of red-breasted merganser 1952–75*

		1952–61	1961–66	1966–71	1971–75
Medway Estuary (S)	Regular	15	21	9	26
	Max	50	60	24	58
Medway Estuary (N)	Regular	—	—	—	—
	Max	—	—	12	1
Thames	Regular	40	20	6	—
	Max	180	48	18	13
Swale	Regular	75	46	34	33
	Max	155	120	60	66
Total of regular counts		130	87	49	59

From earlier records, it is apparent that red-breasted mergansers were seldom seen on the Thames and then only in small numbers, while on the Medway they were rather more often seen, but a party of eleven in January 1947 was noteworthy. A party of eighty was seen on the Swale in December 1947.

Winter visitors arrive from mid-October, very rarely in late September. During the past twenty years, there has been a number of records of one or two birds lingering on into mid-summer and full courtship is now regularly recorded on the Medway each spring. Drakes in full moult have been found on both the Medway and Swale in summer and it must be possible that a pair will eventually breed.

OCCASIONAL VISITORS

Whooper Swan

The whooper swan has always been uncommon in North Kent and is now far outnumbered by the Bewick's swan. The earliest mention

62. Red-breasted merganser.

is in H. L. Mayer's *Coloured Illustrations of British Birds and Their Eggs* in which it is stated that 'in October of the present year, 1848, many were killed about Gravesend', which, if correct, is exceptionally early. On 15th February, 1879, one was shot on the Medway and in December 1893, nine were seen off Whitstable and an injured one captured. One other early record is of one taken in Grovehurst Decoy.

In the present century, Norman Ticehurst saw ten in a blizzard over the Swale on 3rd January, 1904 and it was not until 3rd March, 1946 that the next were reported by G. B. Rimes, four over Murston. Then in February 1947 during severe weather, one was seen on the Medway and seven by Yantlet Creek, followed shortly by one at Cliffe and two at Windmill Creek, which may have been from this party.

With the more intensive observations, whoopers have now been positively identified in seventeen of the past twenty-three years, totalling ninety-nine individuals, the two largest herds both numbering eleven, the first at Cliffe on 21st December, 1952 and the second at Windmill Creek on the exceptionally late date of 2nd April, 1956. The hard winters of 1947, 1956 and 1963 obviously produced weather migrants.

Table 51: *Number of individual whooper swans 1952–74*

	1952	1954	1955	1956	1957	1958	1959	1960	1961
Medway	—	—	—	8	—	—	—	3	—
Thames	11	—	—	—	—	3	1	—	7
Swale	—	1	1	11	5	—	4	—	—
Total	11	1	1	19	5	3	5	3	7

	1962	1963	1965	1968	1969	1970	1972	1974	Total
Medway	—	3	6	—	—	3	—	2	25
Thames	—	4	—	—	7	3	4	2	42
Swale	1	4	—	5	—	—	—	—	32
Total	1	11	6	5	7	6	4	4	99

Table 52: *Monthly occurrences of whooper swans 1952–74*

Jan	Feb	Mar	Apr	Oct	Nov	Dec
22	16	15	11	2	3	32

Bean Goose

The early records of bean geese in much of Western Europe are confused, as there were many instances of mis-identification between this and the pink-footed goose.

Our first definite record is of one at Yantlet Creek from 17th November to 3rd December, 1939. Since 1953, this goose has been identified more regularly (in ten out of twenty-three years) which may only indicate more efficient observing. However, there was a remarkable influx in 1961. Almost all have been seen on the Thames.

Table 53: *Number of individual bean geese 1953–73*

	1953	1956	1958	1960	1961	1963	1967	1968	1971	1973	Total
Medway	—	—	—	—	4	—	—	—	—	—	4
Thames	2	1	2	1	34	1	1	3	1	6	52
Swale	—	—	—	—	1	4	—	1	—	—	6
Total	2	1	2	1	39	5	1	4	1	6	62

Monthly totals show that February is by far the most likely month to see bean geese and their occurrence is probably related to hard weather on the continent, particularly in southern Sweden where large numbers of the forest bean goose winter. Their visits to North Kent are usually brief.

Table 54: *Monthly occurrences of bean geese*

Jan	Feb	March	Dec
5	56	1	5

Field descriptions obtained indicate that all except three belong to the long-billed forest bean goose race. Curiously the short-billed tundra bean goose which winters in large numbers in Holland and Belgium has only once been identified in North Kent, three being seen on the Thames on 24th February, 1976.

Pink-footed Goose

This goose was first identified in the winter of 1906/7, when thirty-four frequented the Leysdown marshes on Sheppey. The next record was in mid-February 1940, when 150 were present at Cliffe, increasing to 200 in early March. Twelve more appeared there in October 1946 and forty in late December, followed by five in March 1947. In mid-January 1949 there were eighteen at Shellness, seven being seen nearby in late February, probably the same birds. Rather smaller numbers have been seen since, but rather more regularly (as with visits by observers), their totals being as follows:

Table 55: *Number of individuals pink-footed goose 1966–74*

	1906-7	1940	1946	1947	1949	1951	1954	1955	1956	1958	1959
Medway	—	—	—	—	—	—	1	—	4	—	5
Thames	—	200	52	5	—	—	1	5	50	—	5
Swale	34	—	—	—	18	1	—	—	—	43	—
Total	34	200	52	5	18	1	2	5	54	43	10

	1960	1961	1962	1963	1964	1965	1967	1968	1969	1970	1973
Medway	—	—	—	—	—	—	—	—	29	—	—
Thames	29	1	—	2	2	2	—	1	15	1	2
Swale	17	30	1	3	47	—	1	—	1	—	—
Total	46	31	1	5	49	2	1	1	45	1	2

	1974	Total
Medway	2	41
Thames	—	373
Swale	—	196
Total	2	610

Monthly occurrences show that the majority occur in February as with the bean and white-fronted goose:

Table 56: *Monthly occurrence of pink-footed geese 1940–74*

Jan	Feb	Mar	Oct	Dec
154	333	266	12	52

The great majority of pinkfeet have been seen with white-fronted geese, which suggests that they are more likely to be of the Spitzbergen population, which have joined the Russian whitefronts on the winter grounds in the Low Countries, rather than Icelandic. Their food preference in North Kent is for grass and they have not been recorded on winter wheat, late stubbles or potatoes, which are more favoured by Icelandic than Spitzbergen birds. However, Icelandic pinkfeet, which winter mainly in North Britain, do reach Kent occasionally, for a Scottish-ringed bird has been shot on the Isle of Sheppey. After a post-war decline in those wintering regularly on the Wash and North Norfolk, their numbers are increasing again and possibly we shall see a corresponding increase in Kentish occurrences.

Snow Goose

Two blue-phase lesser snow geese were seen on the Isle of Sheppey from 18th–22nd February, 1969. As they allowed close approach they were almost certainly feral. Another first year white-phase bird was present on Chetney from 18th–22nd May, 1971. We considered that this was also a lesser snow goose and in contrast to the Sheppey birds, it was comparatively shy, unringed and in perfect condition.

An adult greater snow goose was present on the Medway from May 1972 until November, when it was found dead and the race confirmed. Another greater snow goose was present there in mid-1974 and was perhaps one of the two seen at Shellness on 2nd January or the single bird at Graveney from 1st–7th January.

Canada Goose

Although much more a goose of freshwater lakes than estuaries and brackish marshland, the Canada goose is now starting to colonise the North Kent Marshes.

63. A lesser snow goose photographed on Chetney in 1971.

A flock of thirty-one seen by L. Parmenter on 11th February, 1940 in hard weather, was the first record, one being seen in 1941 and 1948. A small influx took place in 1961 on the Medway, five being seen from February to April. Seven flew north-east over Gillingham on 6th August and fourteen were seen at Faversham that winter. Next summer nine adults and four young were found at Oare, followed by two pairs nesting at Murston in 1963 and one pair in 1964. Scattered birds were seen in the next three years, including nine at Cliffe in October 1966.

A pair at Cliffe pools in the autumn of 1967 was the last sighting until the autumn of 1972 when a maximum of thirty occurred on Barksore followed by three at Cliffe and two on the Swale in April 1973 and a maximum of twenty on the South Medway in the winter in 1974/75, where one pair bred in the following spring.

All records appear to be the introduced Atlantic Canada goose and there is no suggestion of any genuine migrants.

Barnacle Goose

Barnacle geese have always been uncommon in North Kent, although it was known as an irregular visitor to the Swale between 1865–1883 and a gaggle of about forty wintered there regularly during the 1914–18 war. A further twelve were seen on the South Medway on 27th December, 1923, and another was shot there in 1926. Seven were seen on the Swale in February 1948.

Since 1953, barnacles have become more regular as the table shows:

Table 57: *Number of individual barnacle geese 1953–71*

	1953	1954	1955	1958	1958	1959	1961	1962
Medway	—	—	5	8	—	—	12	2
Thames	1	5	—	—	18	6	—	—
Swale	—	9	1	—	20	—	—	2
Total	1	14	6	8	38	6	12	4

	1963	1969	1971	Total
Medway	30	1	—	58
Thames	—	—	—	30
Swale	22	—	1	55
Total	52	1	1	143

The monthly figures show that February is by far the most favoured month:

Table 58: *Monthly occurrences of barnacle geese 1953–71*

Nov	Dec	Jan	Feb	Mar
11	13	38	100	14

In the four mild winters since 1971, the only barnacles seen have been four known to be feral on Barksore. The other figures strongly suggest that those barnacles seen are winter visitors, influenced at times (as in 1963) by severe weather in Europe. This suggests that these are from the Siberian population wintering in Holland and Belgium.

Those seen in North Kent graze mainly the close cropped sheep pastures, particularly on Chetney, for all the Medway records are from this one area. The bird seen on the Swale in 1971 was in company with brent and was grazing on *Zostera*. It had earlier been seen with brent at Leigh-on-Sea, Essex.

Ruddy Shelduck

One, shot on the Medway at the turn of the century, is in the possession of Mr George Webb of Tunstall. Another was shot on the North Kent Marshes on 17th August, 1943, being recorded by T. C. Gregory. An adult drake, seen at Cliffe by E. H. Gillham and L. C. Batchelor for a month from 30th April, 1950 was much more shy than the accompanying shelduck.

An adult duck, first seen on the Inner Thames at Swanscombe on 28th April, 1967, moved to the Medway at Chetney and Stoke between 2nd–6th May, before returning to the Thames at High Halstow, where it was last seen by E. Pithers on 22nd May. It is interesting that this bird's arrival coincided with an influx of white storks into South-East England, during long spells of easterly weather.

In 1973, a female was seen on the Thames at Cliffe on 20th February and again on 22nd September. Another, at Motney Hill on the Medway Estuary on 2nd December could have been the same bird, which also applies to the female at Cliffe intermittently from 19th January–29th April, 1974. These records also link up with sightings from the Inner Thames.

While the possibility of escapes cannot be ruled out, it is possible that some, particularly the first four could be genuinely wild birds.

American Wigeon

There are two records from this area, a young drake seen by J. Hori on Windmill Creek, Sheppey on 10th October, 1961 and a drake on Stoke lagoon, Medway Estuary on 27th April 1968, seen by C. E. Wheeler, P. J. Oliver and R. J. Elvy. Although the possibility of escapes cannot be excluded, the increasing number of records in such places as Ireland renders the genuineness of the Kentish birds equally possible.

201

American Black Duck

One, thought to be a drake, was present on Yantlet Creek and Stoke lagoon from 18th–25th March, 1967, where it was identified by C. E. Wheeler, P. J. Oliver and A. M. Hutson. This was only the second record for the British Isles of this American species, the first being in Eire.

Red-crested Pochard

There are four records from our area, as follows: a drake at Lower Hope Point on 25th November, 1961, another at Capel Fleet on 28th April, 1968 and at Cliffe on 7th February, 1971. Another was seen that year at Windmill Creek on 16th July.

There is increasing evidence for believing that at least some of the records of Kentish red-crested pochard are genuine immigrants from the continent, perhaps from Holland, where this fine duck is slowly increasing and breeding. Thus on 29th October, 1974, during a large scale migration of wildfowl moving off Thanet, a drake red-crested pochard was identified among them.

King Eider

A first winter drake was seen close inshore at Shellness, Sheppey on 27th December, 1955 by J. J. Carr and K. H. Palmer.

Long-tailed Duck

The earliest record was one shot on the Medway prior to 1887, while the second was shot there by Prentis on 28th November, 1887. Singles were then recorded from Gillingham next October, the Swale in November 1902 and then thirty-five years later, two in Yantlet Creek on 10th January, 1947. Three were seen on the Thames on 21st November, 1948, three more there on 7th November, 1949 and one on the Swale on 5th November, 1950.

With the increased birdwatching, post war records have shown long-tailed ducks to be far more regular, having occurred in sixteen of the past twenty-two years, with a total of ninety individuals.

The long-tailed duck is an offshore sea duck in winter and Kent is just within its southern range, where its occurrences in our area are mainly in the Thames or at the wide eastern end of the Swale Channel, less often in the Medway with its narrow mouth. Monthly occurrences show it to be a winter visitor with strong evidence of a

Table 59: *Number of individual long-tailed duck 1955–74*

	1955	1956	1957	1958	1959	1960	1961	1962
Medway	—	—	2	—	—	—	—	—
Thames	1	2	7	3	16	2	3	10
Swale	—	—	2	3	—	2	—	—
Total	1	2	11	6	16	4	3	10

	1963	1964	1965	1967	1969	1972	1973	1974	Total
Medway	—	2	—	—	—	2	2	3	11
Thames	5	—	1	—	3	6	3	—	62
Swale	1	—	1	1	3	1	2	1	17
Total	6	2	2	1	6	9	7	4	90

late autumn passage, but no evidence of any hard weather influence. Storms are more significant. The largest party seen was eight in Egypt Bay in November 1959.

Table 60: *Monthly occurrences of long-tailed duck since 1887*

Jan	Feb	Mar	Apr	Oct	Nov	Dec
24	14	10	6	17	68	29

While the paucity of early records must be disregarded, it is interesting to note that the average number of individuals seen annually in the decade 1953–62 was 5·2; in the subsequent twelve year period, it had fallen to 3·0, which may well be a reflection of oil pollution mortality elsewhere. This duck is highly gregarious in winter and there have been a number of disasters during this time, usually in the Baltic, in which over 10,000 long-tails have been killed at one time.

Of the ninety individuals now recorded, only five have been adult drakes, including the latest spring record – one on a Sheppey fleet on 20th April, 1957. In addition an adult drake, already in full summer plumage, was seen on the South Medway on 18th February, 1975.

Surf Scoter

Two were seen by A. B. Farr at the mouth of the Thames during one of the winters 1875–80. He was able to sail close enough to see their distinguishing features.

Velvet Scoter

Writing in 1953, James Harrison listed the twenty-four known occurrences, fourteen from the Thames, seven from the Medway and three from the Swale. There is also a record of 'large numbers' seen at sea off Sheerness on 11th January, 1944. This area is now scarcely watched and although not within the North Kent Marshes, it is a possible origin of those which move into our area.

It is now possible to make a reasonably accurate assessment of the number of individuals which have been sighted annually from 1952–1974 and there is no doubt that velvet scoters have increased and have tended to favour the eastern Swale more than the Thames, particularly in the past seven years, but apart from this, there are no obvious trends.

Table 61: *Number of individual velvet scoter*

	1952	1953	1954	1955	1956	1957	1958	1959	Total
Medway	1	2	1	2	1	—	—	—	7
Thames	—	5	2	7	16	15	11	5	61
Swale	4	—	4	2	25	6	18	—	59
Total	5	7	7	11	42	21	29	5	127

	1960	1961	1962	1963	1964	1965	1966	1967	Total
Medway	—	—	1	2	—	—	—	2	5
Thames	1	9	15	11	—	6	2	2	46
Swale	6	31	9	6	5	5	8	—	70
Total	7	40	25	19	5	11	10	4	121

	1968	1969	1970	1971	1972	1973	1974	Total	Overall Total
Medway	—	—	—	—	—	—	—	—	12
Thames	5	2	—	—	9	—	1	17	124
Swale	7	16	15	7	26	15	9	95	224
Total	12	18	15	7	35	15	10	112	360

The monthly occurrences show that the velvet scoter is a winter visitor, the earliest record being 7th September, 1956 and the latest 6th April, 1957. Like the long-tailed duck there appears to be a marked autumn passage with a peak in November. The only summer record is one drake seen by C. E. Wheeler off the mouth of the Swale on 31st July, 1971.

Table 62: *Monthly occurrences (all records)*

Jan	Feb	Mar	Apr	July	Sept	Oct	Nov	Dec
36	21	33	6	1	2	77	144	55

There is no evidence of any increase in hard weather, but a small increase during spring passage. A number of records, sadly, are of birds weakened from oil pollution.

Smew

In 1909, Ticehurst considered that 'red head' smews (ducks and young drakes) were almost annual winter visitors to the Kentish estuaries and particularly to the Thames. Writing in 1950, Gillham and Homes found it far less regular. Prior to 1939 they only knew of three periods in which smews had been seen and then only 'red heads'. Since 1952, it has become regular again in small numbers, being seen in twenty-two out of the past twenty-three years.

Table 63: *Numbers of individual smews 1940–74*

	1940	1946	1947	1948	1952	1953	1954	1955	1956	1957
Medway	—	2	8	—	—	—	6	4	2	—
Thames	1	—	—	—	8	11	17	18	42	14
Swale	—	—	7	1	3	—	4	4	3	—
Total	1	2	15	1	11	11	27	26	47	14

	1958	1959	1960	1961	1962	1963	1964	1966	1967	1968
Medway	—	1	2	1	1	11	4	—	—	—
Thames	2	3	—	10	3	12	—	1	1	1
Swale	1	—	—	—	1	—	—	3	—	—
Total	3	4	2	11	5	23	4	4	1	1

	1969	1970	1971	1972	1973	1974	Total
Medway	2	2	1	1	—	1	49
Thames	2	—	1	2	—	1	150
Swale	2	—	—	—	2	—	31
Total	6	2	2	3	2	2	230

Clearly the Thames is by far the most favoured locality, the great majority of sightings being on Cliffe Pools and it can be assumed that many of these birds had been moving to and from winter quarters on London's reservoirs. It is interesting to note that during the decade

1952–61 there were almost three times as many records as in the twelve-year period since.

During the 1940–74 period, only sixty-seven adult males were seen, exactly twenty-nine per cent, which compares closely with the goosander figures from North Kent and with an estimate of twenty-five to thirty-three per cent of adult drake smews from London's reservoirs. Our North Kent figures were considerably raised, however, by the fact that no less than forty of the adult drakes were seen on only two occasions, namely twenty-eight adult drakes out of thirty-five on Cliffe Pools on 4th February, 1956 and a party of twelve flying offshore there on 22nd December, 1957.

The smew is a species in which there is a marked segregation of adult drakes from 'red heads' in mid-winter. On the Elbe Estuary in Germany, JGH found the population of adult drakes reached a peak of eighty-five per cent in January, whereas on the Ijsselmeer in Holland in January, there was only seventeen per cent of adult drakes. A likely explanation would seem to be that the ducks and young are less hardy and therefore move further south-west along the European flyway. Hard weather definitely increases the incidence of smews.

Goosander

The goosander remains an irregular winter visitor, perhaps rather more often observed with the increased birdwatching of the past twenty-five years. However, wintering goosanders favour enclosed waters such as reservoirs, so that Cliffe Pools, Murston clay pits and the embanked Windmill Creek, relatively new man-made habitat, have certainly played their parts in this increase.

Many of the other records are of birds on the move in autumn, including the largest party of all, fourteen flying west past Shellness on 31st October, 1963. An adult drake was seen arriving there from the north-east on 25th November, 1972 in company with twelve red-breasted mergansers. Others have been seen moving west up the Thames past Allhallows and south-west over Rochester in November and December. These must be birds moving from the Low Countries to inland waters, such as the London reservoirs.

Up to 1952, there were only fifteen dated occurrences the most being a party of seven on the Medway. From 1952–74, it has been possible to assess the number of individuals which now total 106. The recent decade of mild winters has seen a fall off in numbers, but goosanders have been seen in seventeen out of the past twenty-three years.

Table 64: *Number of individual goosanders 1953–74*

	1953	1954	1955	1956	1957	1958	1959	1960	1961	1962	1963
Medway	—	1	1	1	—	4	1	—	4	1	6
Thames	1	1	6	—	2	4	8	3	5	1	9
Swale	—	—	—	—	—	6	—	2	1	1	15
Total	1	2	7	1	2	14	9	5	10	3	30

	1964	1967	1968	1969	1972	1974	Total
Medway	3	—	2	—	—	—	24
Thames	2	3	4	—	—	—	49
Swale	1	—	1	3	1	2	33
Total	6	3	7	3	1	2	106

The monthly occurrences show that there is virtually no hard weather influence in North Kent except in 1963. This is because our area is almost always within the weather system initiating such migrations. Of the 106 individuals detailed, thirty (28·3%) were adult drakes, which supports the view that females and young migrate further south-west in winter than the tougher adult drakes, a differential migration which is also marked in smews.

Table 65: *Monthly occurrences of goosanders 1953–74*

Jan	Feb	Mar	Apr	May	Oct	Nov	Dec
18	24	14	2	1	15	20	21

The latest date was a female on Cliffe Fleet on 12th May, 1937.

CHAPTER 7

FROM TILBURY TO FOULNESS

꧁꧂

THIS section of the Thames extends eastwards from Tilbury to Foulness Point, a distance of just over thirty miles. With the deep water channel lying close inshore, the saltmarsh and intertidal zone is at first limited to a narrow stretch of about two miles mainly to the west of Mucking Creek, known as East Tilbury flats, an area which at times holds sizeable flocks of wildfowl, but these are often only on brief visits from the Kentish shore and its importance is rapidly declining.

The western end of Sea Reach is dominated by the great oil refineries and petrochemical complexes at Thameshaven and Canvey Island on both sides of Holehaven Creek. A branch of this – Easthaven Creek – joins Benfleet Creek which runs in from the east and thus separates Canvey Island from the mainland.

From the mid-point of Canvey the main channel of Sea Reach moves out into the centre of the estuary, so that a massive intertidal zone is uncovered at low tide from here eastwards, known as Chapman Sands off Canvey Point, continuing eastward as Southend Flat, around Shoeburyness to Maplin Sands off Foulness Island, merging with Foulness Sand, which divides the Thames Estuary from the mouth of the Crouch.

EAST TILBURY FLATS

The saltmarsh to the immediate north of Coalhouse Fort extends for over a mile, but is now too narrow to hold substantial numbers of fowl. At low tide considerably more extensive mudflats are uncovered and these are quite often used as a low tide roost by dabbling duck, many of which have crossed from the Kentish side. This is also the case with diving duck seen in the river, which are from Cliffe Pools. It is possible, however, that gravel extractions creating flooded pits just inland of the sea wall may in due course come to hold sizeable flocks of diving duck. The Warren pits already hold almost fifty tufted duck and rather fewer pochard.

The saltmarsh here is composed mainly of red fescue and sea couch grass, sea aster and sea purslane. Marked tidal erosion is occurring and it is a pity that these saltmarshes cannot be grazed, for the grass is too long to attract wigeon. However, it is interesting to note that this saltmarsh supports more sea aster than anywhere on the North Kent Marshes. Greenhalgh (1975) has recorded both sea aster and sea purslane as popular pintail foods on the Ribble and it could well be that the pintail seen at East Tilbury were feeding on these saltings at night, although this was not proved. Saltmarsh is absent on either side of Mucking Creek and minimal just further east before Thameshaven.

The land to the immediate west of Mucking Creek consists of a massive tip for refuse brought down from London by river. For anyone wishing to get an idea of what the implications are for the north Medway, if Stoke Saltings became a GLC refuse tip, a visit to Mucking is essential – and frightening.

Furthermore, the refuse is unloaded by crane from flat-bottomed lighters which merely come alongside the sea wall and rise and fall with each tide. Inevitably, as the grabs unload the lighters into lorries an unacceptable amount of refuse is dropped into the Thames to be carried by the winds and tides to litter the tideline. Both shores of the Thames are being polluted in this way by virtually indestructable plastic and other filth. The whole unloading operation is a disgrace which should be controlled by the construction of proper unloading bays where refuse spillage cannot escape into the estuary.

However, perhaps this area could one day serve as a site for another oil refinery if it is still required. How much better it would be here rather than on the Kentish side at Cliffe, for at Mucking it would merely be an extension of the adjoining Thameshaven.

Records of wildfowl (excluding diving duck on the river) on this stretch of the Essex Thames are shown in the table.

Decreases in the principle species, mallard, teal, wigeon, pintail and shelduck are marked, probably the result of disturbance from refuse disposal at Mucking, together with saltmarsh erosion at East Tilbury, which has apparently now rendered the area too small for pintail, for not one has been recorded in the past six seasons. This is a sad change from the peak count of 840 made on 31st December,

1960. Some, of course, may now be wintering on the Inner Thames, while decreases have coincided with increases on the Essex Stour.

Table 66: *Wildfowl counts: Tilbury to Thameshaven 1954–75*

		1954–62	1962–69		1969–75	
Mallard	Regular	425	42		293	(1973–74 and
	Max	1000	300		338	1974–75 only)
Teal	Regular	15	—		—	
	Max	130	46		4	
Wigeon	Regular	100	—		—	
	Max	530	37		54	
Pintail	Regular	235	117	(1st four	—	
	Max	500	800	seasons only)	—	
Shoveler	Regular	—	—		—	
	Max	—	30		4	
Shelduck	Regular	345	288	(Four seasons	166	(1973–74 and
	Max	1215	800	only)	297	1974–75 only)
Brent	Regular	—	—		—	
	Max	—	15		—	
Mute Swan	Regular	5	—		—	
	Max	25	39		23	

Over fifty years ago, according to an eighty-year-old local wildfowler, small numbers of white-fronted geese regularly used to feed on the marshes that then existed around Mucking Creek, Thameshaven and Canvey. Occasional wandering skeins still flight over East Tilbury from their north Kent stronghold, but the area can no longer accommodate them for feeding – a warning of what could easily happen in north Kent.

Other notable records include a party of twenty long-tailed duck in December 1957, part of an influx, for thirty were also recorded in that month on the Naze. A female velvet scoter was seen on the moat of Coalhouse Fort on 12th March, 1961, two more at East Tilbury on 29th January, 1966 and an eider off Mucking Creek on 20th December, 1959. Twelve whooper swans were seen at East Tilbury on 15th March, 1959 and four others on 15th January, 1960.

A unique record is of fifty brent feeding on flooded fields at Hainault, sixteen miles west-north-west of the nearest tidal flats at Mucking on 8th March, 1967. Even nowadays, with brent feeding inland in large concentrations, this is a remarkable distance from the coast – and over thirty miles away from the nearest concentrations of brent.

FROM TILBURY TO FOULNESS

LEIGH MARSH AND CANVEY POINT

The intertidal flats surrounding Canvey Point and Two Tree Island are enclosed from the west by the industrial and urban developments on Canvey and are overlooked by hills to the north, and by Leigh-on-Sea with its picturesque waterfront and the massive buildings of Southend and its pier beyond.

Extensive saltmarshes, similar botanically to those already described on the Medway, extend along the southern and eastern sides of Two Tree Island and over a considerable area of Canvey Point. The intertidal flats are predominantly sandy with a shallow layer of overlying mud. This supports extensive beds of eel-grass, which grows particularly well around the eastern and southern shores of Two Tree Island and the mouth of Leigh Creek.

Work by the Institute of Terrestrial Ecology has shown that the eel-grass bed at Leigh has increased from a minimum area of 8·4 hectares in 1953 to 95·6 hectares in September 1974. The two species *Zostera marina* and *Z. noltii* are growing together, but with the former in the wetter depressions and the latter on the hummocks.

In December 1974, the Leigh National Nature Reserve was declared, covering 634 acres including the saltmarshes of Two Tree Island and a large area of the mudflats. The need for a reserve here had become obvious by 1967 for several reasons. First and foremost, the area had become a major resort for brent interchanging frequently with Foulness, which was, of course, under threat of total destruction for London's third airport and Maplin seaport. Also, there were at that time plans for a major roadway which would have been constructed along the shore. Finally, 'marsh cowboys' from East London were roaming the area shooting anything which flew, including brent.

By 1968, development plans were abandoned and the Leigh-on-Sea Wildfowlers' Association, the Essex Naturalists' Trust and the Southend Council devised a plan whereby Two Tree Island was declared a reserve managed by the Essex Trust and the Leigh WA took over the shooting rights on the tidal foreshore, their wildfowling taking place between 1600 hours and 0900 hours next morning.

Their main quarry species is the wigeon, which feeds on the eel-grass beds with the brent. Under this new regime, the 'marsh cowboys' have been eliminated, responsible wildfowlers have enjoyed some good wigeon flighting and both brent and wigeon

211

64. Brent geese off Two Tree Island with Leigh-on-Sea in the background.

numbers using the area have shown substantial increases. With the declaration of the National Nature Reserve in 1974, the same arrangement continues.

Leigh-on-Sea must be the most remarkable place for observing brent anywhere in England. Not only can they be seen feeding among the anchored boats off Two Tree and in Leigh Creek, but in the late winter, when the *Zostera* is eaten out, those few hundred that remain move right in under the water front, taking no notice of the electric trains which noisily pass by, often a mere thirty yards away, as the geese search out the sea lettuce which becomes their staple diet here in late winter.

Not only do the brent move between Leigh and Foulness, but they also move across to Canvey Point and the same applies to wigeon. On spring tides both species also feed on the flooded higher saltmarsh grasses on Two Tree Island and Canvey.

Wildfowl counts over the past twenty years summarised in the table show how Leigh marsh has become an increasingly important and spectacular wildfowl resort.

Table 67: *Wildfowl counts: Leigh Marsh 1955–75*

		1955–56 to 1961–62	1962–63 to 1968–69	1969–70 to 1974–75
Mallard	Regular	—	—	53
	Max	40	6	140
Teal	Regular	—	—	—
	Max	100	61	155
Wigeon	Regular	300	819	1173
	Max	700	1898	2716
Pintail	Regular	—	—	—
	Max	5	7	12
Shelduck	Regular	30	72	50
	Max	100	348	178
Brent goose	Regular	300*	1373*	3251*
	Max	845	2434	5500

* Average annual peak.

It is interesting to note how the return of the eel-grass at Leigh has been followed by most encouraging increases in both brent and wigeon. There is undoubtedly competition between these two species for the available supplies of this food and it is usually largely eaten out by mid-December, after which both show substantial decreases as they move elsewhere.

It is also instructive to note how mallard and teal are tending to increase since the area became properly controlled. Leigh is, however, basically an eel-grass marsh so far as wildfowl are concerned, so the species range is limited. Other wildfowl do occur from time to time, of course, of which the following are most notable:

Eider: 138 off Southend in January 1963 is the largest flock ever seen in Essex.

Snow goose: Two on 13th and 18th April, 1911.

Red-breasted goose: One adult with the brent from mid-October to 7th November, 1975, having been seen earlier in October with brent at Foulness. This bird fed on eel-grass and saltmarsh

213

65 & 66. The red-breasted goose that joined the brent at Two Tree Island in 1975.

grasses at full tide; when feeding on the latter, it grazed far more rapidly than the brent. Both species nest in close proximity in Arctic Siberia, so it is perhaps surprising that only one other red-breasted goose has ever been found with the brent – one shot on Ray Sands off the Dengie coast on 6th January, 1871. Winter food preferences of red-breasted geese are the obvious ecological barrier, being growing cereals and freshmarsh grass.

Barnacle goose: One with the brent from 27th December, 1969 to 4th January, 1970.

Light-breasted brent goose: Three among the Russian brent on 16th January, 1969 and two on 18th January, 1970.

Finally, there is another lesson to be learnt at Leigh, for the wildfowl have become quite used to the comings and goings of the fishing boats and the various sailing activities, although the latter admittedly are on a greatly reduced scale in winter. However, even the occasional speed boats using the outer part of Benfleet Creek are tolerated down to ranges of about 250 yards.

67. Restless brent at high tide off Two Tree Island.

THE NORTH KENT MARSHES AND THE SOUTH ESSEX SHORE

The peninsula of Foulness lies between the estuaries of the Thames and the Crouch. It consists of a series of low-lying islands, Potton, Rushy, Havengore and New England Islands to the south-west with Foulness Island forming the main part of the peninsula to the north-east. Much of this land was embanked from the sea before the year 1400.

Between 1900–1918, the Ministry of Defence gradually acquired control of the area and of the massive intertidal zone of Maplin and Foulness Sands for its armament research. It was here, in the 1930's, that Air Marshal Sir Ralph Sorley, uncle of JGH, then a Squadron Leader working with the Air Staff's Operational Requirements, developed the eight-gun fighter aircraft concept and shot to pieces an old aircraft with eight Browning guns firing in short bursts. In so doing, he was able to convince Sydney Camm, designer of the Hurricane and Reginald Mitchell, designer of the Spitfire of the necessity of their two now immortal aircraft having eight guns.

So, while we may express disappointment at the restricted access

68. A light-breasted brent goose off Two Tree Island in 1970.

for birdwatchers on Foulness, it is as well to remember that some of the seeds of victory in the Battle of Britain were indeed sown here and many other research projects that proved vital for our survival.

Also, because of the MOD presence, a large area of land has been taken out of arable use and has reverted to a varied grassland flora providing important roosting, nesting and other habitats for birds. Few other areas can rival Foulness for the extent of its brackish grassland and the lack of disturbance. At high tide in mid-winter up to 50,000 wading birds flight to roost on these grasslands and the open arable on New England and Havengore Islands from their intertidal feeding grounds far out on Maplin and Foulness Sands, which hold the most important wader concentrations in South-east England.

There are no extensive areas of saltmarsh in the Foulness area, but a narrow belt runs north-eastwards from the mid-point of Foulness Island and just encircles Foulness Point. Although this saltmarsh totals no more than fifty hectares, it is of national importance as it supports the largest remaining area of pure cord grass, *Spartina maritima*, in Britain and probably Europe. This was one of the parent species of *Spartina anglica*, a hybrid now commonly found throughout saltmarshes in Britain and used for land reclamation. Foulness Point itself is composed of the largest cockle bank in Britain and is an important nesting site for little and common terns and ringed plovers. There is also an important wader tide roost here.

The intertidal zone of Maplin and Foulness Sands is separated from the low lying land by a sea wall with the narrow belt of salting beyond. The flats extend for ten miles and the tide ebbs for about three miles, uncovering 10,500 hectares of sandbanks at low tide. The only soft mud is a narrow strip just offshore of the saltings. It is interesting to note that although this area was found to be rich in wader foods when surveyed recently by Dr D. G. Kay and R. Knight, the mollusc *Hydrobia ulvae*, laver spire shell, represented only 1·3 per cent of the biomass, and as this is the principle food of shelduck and to a lesser extent pintail, this would account for their relative scarcity compared with the Medway, where the intertidal fauna was dominated by this mollusc, which reached densities approaching 20,000 per square metre at several sites.

The *Zostera* beds on Maplin start at Foulness Point and extend south-westwards just over five miles to the mouth of Havengore Creek, with a further bed lying between Wakering Stairs and Pig's Bay. The maximum width of the former is about 400 yards and the latter 250 yards, the great majority of the northern bed being *Z. noltii* (185 hectares), whereas *Z. marina* covers only three hectares. The southern bed is made up of fifty-six hectares of *Z. noltii* and fifty-five hectares of *Z. marina*. Patches of green seaweeds (*Enteromorpha*) are found between the saltings and the start of the *Zostera* beds. These massive *Zostera* beds have, of course, provided the main food for brent geese and wigeon, Maplin being the main arrival and feeding area in Britain for up to twenty per cent of the world's population of the Russian or dark-bellied brent.

The status of this goose has given rise to grave concern since the 1930's, when its main food, at that time *Zostera marina*, was largely destroyed by a mycetozoan disease. When this happened, brent did not adapt as did wigeon to alternative foods and consequently suffered a serious decline, estimated at about seventy-five per cent of their numbers.

By 1960, the world population was approximately 18,000, increasing to about 30,000 in 1966 and from 34,000 in the winter of 1971–72 to a remarkable peak of almost 80,000 in 1973–74. A bad breeding season in 1974 caused a slight drop and then a further excellent season in 1975 saw the population reach 100,000.

69. Wigeon jump at the top of the tide.

Maplin and Foulness Sands are therefore of immense international importance for their brent geese and wader populations. As already mentioned, it is unfortunate from the data view point that Foulness has only been subjected to limited observer cover, which is not comparable to that on the North Kent Marshes. Nevertheless regular counts have been made by permit holders and more recently by those working for the Department of the Environment. The following tables are based on the wildfowl count data held by the Wildfowl Trust.

Table 68: *Regular and maximum wildfowl counts in the Foulness area, 1962–75. A number of other species have occurred, but do not qualify for a Regular figure, some of which certainly would with more observer cover. All available observations are included here as maximum counts*

		Mallard	Teal	Wigeon	Shelduck	Brent goose	Mute swan
1962–68	Regular	193	40	1,070	136	5,838*	60
	Max	622	119	2,460	319	7,074	110
1968–75	Regular	215	119	1,486	263	7,943*	56
	Max	664	318	7,500	525	12,868	136

* Average annual peak.

Maximum wildfowl counts in the Foulness area, 1962–75

	Gadwall	Pintail	Shoveler	Pochard	Tufted	Scaup
1962–68	5	19	5	16	9	6
1968–75	8	60	68	145	53	2

	Goldeneye	Long-tailed duck	Common Scoter	Velvet Scoter	Eider	Red-breasted Merganser
1962–68	1	1	50	1	16	21
1968–75	8	2	610	3	84	12

	White-fronted goose	Greylag goose	Pink-footed goose	Barnacle goose	Canada goose	Whooper swan
1962–68	9	—	20	—	—	5
1968–75	97	12	5	1	43	1

219

In addition to the species listed in the tables, the following must be mentioned:

American wigeon: a first winter drake shot on Foulness Island on 20th December, 1962.

Common scoter: 3,500 were found three miles off Foulness Point on 30th August, 1958, emphasising once again our lack of knowledge of sea duck among the outer sandbanks of the Thames.

Bean goose: one shot on Foulness Island on 24th October, 1936.

Barnacle goose: one seen on Foulness Island on 13th March, 1935 and a maximum of seven between mid-December, 1958 and 24th January, 1959.

Pacific brent goose: one identified at Foulness on 9th and 17th February, 1957 and 8th February, 1958.

Very little has been published on the breeding wildfowl of Foulness, but the Table for 1973 was included in *A Habitat Assessment of the Foulness Area*, published by the Nature Conservancy Council and was based on a survey made by I. Deans:

Table 69: *Number of breeding pairs of wildfowl on Foulness and Potton Islands in 1973*

	Foulness	Potton
Mallard	15	0
Teal	10	0
Gadwall	2	0
Shoveler	2	0
Pochard	2	1
Shelduck	25	4
Mute swan	7	1

THE BATTLE FOR FOULNESS

When the plans for siting London's third airport at Foulness were first publicised, it was natural that conservationists should be extremely worried. The airport itself was to extend from the southern part of Foulness Sand almost to Pig's Bay in the south. New dock facilities for the Port of London were to be sited outside the airport, which would be linked to the North Sea by a new deep water channel capable of taking tankers of up to half a million tons.

If this development came into being, not only would Maplin be destroyed, but a huge area of the Essex coast and the whole of the North Kent Marshes would have been subjected to severe noise pollution.

Initially there were four possible sites for the third London airport, three of them inland. Fortunately the Government set up a commission to assess the merits of those four and quite naturally there was widespread opposition to them all.

In so far as Foulness was concerned, it was the duty of conservationists to produce the evidence to protect the site, so that this could be assessed by the Roskill Commission, which had the unenviable task of sorting out the mass of evidence for and against each of the four sites.

So far as the conservationists were concerned, as Malcolm Ogilvie and Geoffrey Matthews have recorded, the national and local societies concerned with bird conservation showed an unparalleled degree of unanimity of opinion and coordination of action against what they saw as a classical case of the 'wetlands-are-wastelands' approach.

The Army Bird Watching Society, the British Trust for Ornithology, the Essex Bird Watching and Preservation Society, the Essex Joint Council of Wildfowling Clubs, the Essex Naturalists' Trust, the Foulness Wildfowl Counting and Bird Watching Group, the Royal Society for the Protection of Birds, the Seabird Group, the South Essex Natural History Society, the Wildfowlers' Association of Great Britain and Ireland and the Wildfowl Trust joined together to present a reasoned objection at the Public Enquiry.

They were supported by the International Council for Bird Preservation and the International Wildfowl Research Bureau. The IWRB representatives of fifteen nations meeting in Vienna cabled the commission with the request that it should most carefully consider the scientific evidence submitted to it. Letters were also written to the commission by foreign experts in Denmark, Holland and France.

At that time Foulness and Maplin Sands were supporting a fifth of the world population of brent for three months from November to January and the ornithological bodies rightly emphasised the very real risk of aircraft bird strikes from the tens of thousands of wildfowl and waders using the area, not to mention an estimated 180,000 roosting gulls in winter.

If the conservation bodies provided the scientific evidence, then the Defenders of Essex rallied local opinion, brilliantly led by the indefatigable Derek Wood and another local stalwart, Mrs Mollie Drake, later to receive the MBE.

The rest of the saga is now history. The Roskill Commission came out in favour of an inland site – Cublington in Buckinghamshire – but in a minority report Professor R. J. Buchanan gave his reasons for favouring Foulness. The Government then rejected the majority finding and backed Professor Buchanan. In 1973 the Maplin Development Bill went through Parliament but, early in 1974, the whole project was reassessed in view of the fall-off in air traffic following the rising cost of fuel and in June 1974 the project was officially abandoned.

There still remains the problem of the seaport and in May 1974 a scheme for a Maplin 'Seaport Solo' was submitted to the Government by the PLA. No doubt this proposal will be the subject of yet another public enquiry in due course.

It is now suggested to site the proposed Maplin Seaport three miles from Shoeburyness East Beach. The total area required for dock developments to meet forseeable future needs and a possible oil terminal is 607 hectares. The remainder of the enclosed area, excluding any for the Ministry of Defence is about another 607 hectares. Of this, the Essex County Council according to the PLA Report has indicated that a total of 405 hectares is likely to be acceptable as residential or industrial land. It is therefore planned to leave the remainder as a 202 hectare artificial lake between the residential area and the seaport with its adjoining industrial area.

As to the amenities, the PLA points out that the new lake will be of high amenity value, with locks to provide sailors with access to the open sea. The sea defences would be in the form of an attractive curving gravel and sand beach, similar to the trial bank already constructed, $3\frac{1}{2}$ miles in length along the southern boundary.

No conservationist wishes to see any of these unspoiled areas of Maplin Sands destroyed in this way, particularly with the additional risks of pollution from a probable oil terminal.

We are now in the somewhat surprising position of having three possible major dock complexes being suggested – the PLA's Maplin Sea Port, the Medway Ports Authority's Lappel Bank development and Bowater's proposals for dock developments inside the Medway Estuary. The latter is unthinkable for it would utterly devastate the

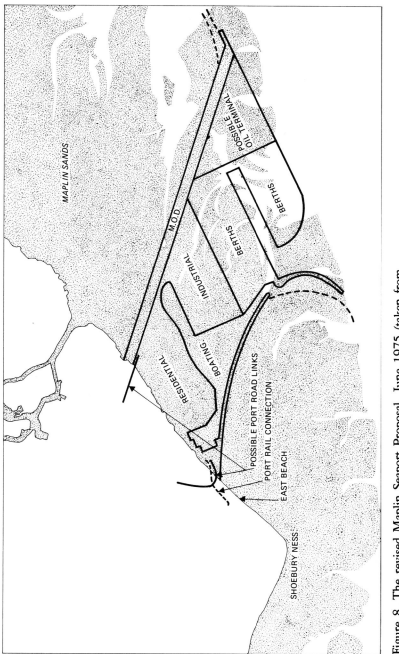

MAPLIN SANDS

M.O.D.

POSSIBLE OIL TERMINAL

BERTHS

BERTHS

INDUSTRIAL

RESIDENTIAL

BOATING

POSSIBLE PORT ROAD LINKS

PORT RAIL CONNECTION

EAST BEACH

SHOEBURY NESS

Figure 8. The revised Maplin Seaport Proposal, June 1975 (taken from the Port of London Authority's 'Revised Preliminary Proposal').

223

Estuary. The other two must surely be considered in the national interest. Do we need both? Without doubt the one which would do the least damage to the natural environment would be that sited on Lappel Bank. If the Maplin Sea Port is decided upon, then with careful planning there could be certain compensations.

One of the happiest outcomes of the Maplin project was the impetus it created for research, financed by the Department of the Environment through contracts organised by the Institute of Terrestrial Ecology, involving the Nature Conservancy Council, the Wildfowl Trust, the British Trust for Ornithology, the Ministry of Agriculture and the Department of Trade and Industry.

One project was on the feeding ecology of the brent goose, carried out by K. Charman. The objective here was to assess the carrying capacities of potential and known brent haunts on the Kent and Essex coasts with a view to their acquisition should the food resources on Maplin be destroyed for LTA.

Following the remarkable increase in numbers in the winter of 1973/74, however, the brent dispersed from Foulness about a month earlier than usual and, quite unexpectedly, a considerable amount of feeding took place on agricultural land inside the sea wall for the first time since the severe winter of 1962/63.

It seems highly likely that the *Zostera* was eaten out a month earlier because of the greatly increased numbers of geese, and under this pressure they took to inland grass and growing cereals remarkably quickly (considering that they never did this in the 1930's) for throughout the latter part of that winter they were feeding in this way in many different parts of Essex – but not as yet in Kent. Grass was slightly more favoured than cereals. By February 1974, probably a quarter of the brent in England were feeding inside the sea walls.

When feeding in the fields, Charman noted that brent on winter wheat on the Dengie were not only more easily disturbed, but were also very much more wary, so that they spent only thirty-four per cent of their time feeding, compared with an average of fifty-nine per cent of time feeding when out on the intertidal flats of the Dengie.

A flock of up to 800 fed on Foulness Island and on the fields along the southern side of the Crouch. Watching these birds, we were immediately struck by their utterly different behaviour compared with those out on the shore. Flying in, they circled several times over their feeding area, giving a marvellous exhibition of mass formation flying. On the fields, they also grazed in close formation, circling as they moved across the field and they tended to move much quicker on winter wheat than grass. When anything alarmed them, such as a distant light aircraft, their necks were all raised and they fanned out, ready for instant take-off, which sometimes happened for no apparent reason.

Perhaps, when they have become acclimatised to inland feeding, this highly nervous type of feeding will be modified. Certainly the inland feeding habit has now become regular and widespread – and at Rye Harbour in Sussex in January 1976, a lone pair of adults was even roosting on a flooded gravel pit nearly a mile from the shore. In the Low Countries inland feeding has been practised for much longer, brent moving inland to graze the 'early bite' high protein grass during spring migration.

A further very instructive pioneering study into the movements of brent geese was carried out by Andrew St Joseph and Tim Bennett of the Wildfowl Trust. On the expiry of the Government's three-year contract at the end of 1974/75, the Wildfowl Trust arranged for the former to continue with his work at least for another winter. This study involved catching and colour marking a total of 817 brent in the three winters 1972/73 (59), 1973/74 (531) and 1974/75 (227). In this way each individual goose can be identified by its large yellow leg ring with black lettering and numbers. This study is focusing on the movements and traditional returns of individual birds, family groups and the behaviour of known pairs and is already providing a wealth of new information.

One other development must be mentioned under Foulness – a thousand-yard stretch of trial sea wall built along the outer margin of Maplin Sands of mixed shingle and sand, forming a natural island at high tide. Up to fifty eiders can be seen in the vicinity and it is possible that a nesting colony could be encouraged here.

Finally, it is instructive to compare the two areas of maximum international importance on the outer Thames – Foulness and the Medway Estuary. Without doubt the diversity and holding capacity of the Medway for wildfowl is far greater than that of Foulness. Both have comparable fresh marshes – Barksore and Chetney on the Medway and the various islands of the Foulness peninsula. Foulness holds no duck species with a status of international importance. The Medway holds five and one is left with the inescapable conclusion that it is the diversity of the Medway's saltmarsh, its islands and intertidal mudflats, which is the vital factor here.

APPENDIX

❦

WATERFOWL FEEDING ON THE THAMES

A report by John Swift, Assistant Director, Conservation and Research, WAGBI.

DURING the winters of 1972/73 and 1973/74, small numbers of waterfowl feeding on the Inner Thames were shot, under licence issued to JS and JGH from the Home Office, through the Nature Conservancy Council. This was done to establish their principal foods on different stretches of the river, as it was apparent that they were not those taken by waterfowl elsewhere and that this could be important in explaining the return of waterfowl to the Thames. Accidentally, we made some interesting observations on plastic pellets, the raw material for manufacturing plastic objects, also commonly used as a packing material, which were taken by ducks in mistake for either grain or grit. These pellets were found floating in the river in astonishing numbers at Putney and were found in duck between the Lower Pool and Rainham.

The foods being taken depended on what was available. In the regions above Dagenham, the animals present in the mudbanks were almost exclusively the extremely abundant *Tubifex* worms. In this region, we found mallard, pintail, teal, shelduck and pochard feeding intensively on them, filtering the mud through their bills and swallowing the *Tubifex* thus extracted. The different species kept mostly to separate areas of mudbank. shelduck and pintail tended to feed further from the shore on slightly stickier mud, which was less easy to filter, but teal fed along the shoreline and up the wet drainage gutters. Pochard would concentrate in shallows or along the tideline seldom allowing themselves to get far from the water. When the tide rose, rafts of duck formed on the river or flighted to nearby waters, such as the disused Surrey Docks, to await the ebb, whereupon they would return as soon as mud was exposed.

226

Mallard were to be found all along the river and most of them fed on *Tubifex*, as far upriver as Putney. Dunlin flight upriver from downstream roosts as soon as the mud becomes exposed, to feed rapidly and inconspicuously on *Tubifex*.

Below Dagenham the animals in the mud were more typically estuarine, the ragworm (*Nereis diversicolor*) becoming extremely abundant. The larger waders are believed to feed on this and JGH and PFH observed the glossy ibis doing so.

Mute swans fed in three different ways. At Silvertown they formed large flocks to feed on grain spillage; but elsewhere they fed either on *Tubifex* or the green algae, *Enteromorpha*. When feeding on *Tubifex* they would either reach beneath the water to the depth of their necks and filter the *Tubifex*, or feed like shelduck on exposed mud.

Tubifex lives in brackish water mud which is low in oxygen. As the Thames has been cleaned up, the oxygen in the riverside mud has increased. The oxygenating effect of the tidal flushing of the river has been able to push the outermost limit of *Tubifex*, a species common to the Thames, gradually further upstream. *Tubifex costatus* (which is the same as found in seawater) can be found in salinities up to thirty-six per cent, if conditions are suitably anaerobic.

The following species were examined with results as shown:

Table 70: *Stomach contents of waterfowl shot on the Inner Thames*

	No.	Tubifex	Green Algae	Plant seeds	Grain	Plastic pellets	Lead shot	Empty
Mallard	15	7	7	2(alder)	4	6	Nil	1
Teal	3	2	2	Nil	Nil	Nil	Nil	1
Pintail	3	3	Nil	Nil	Nil	Nil	Nil	Nil
Pochard	3	2	Nil	Nil	Nil	1	Nil	1
Shelduck	4	2	1	Nil	Nil	Nil	3*	1
Dunlin	9	7	Nil	Nil	Nil	Nil	Nil	2

* Although lead shot was present in the gizzards of three out of four shelduck, this must not be taken as representative, as they were shot because they looked ill. However, like plastic pellets, these shot had probably been taken in mistake for grit.

Once the main foods were definitely established in this way, it was possible to continue the study on field observations alone. Of the thirty-one specimens examined which contained food, seventy-four per cent were found to have been taking *Tubifex*.

GLOSSARY OF
SCIENTIFIC NAMES

❧

BIRDS

The nomenclature in this book follows *The Status of Birds in Britain and Ireland*, British Ornithologists' Union (1971)

Red-throated Diver   *Gavia stellata* (Pontoppidan)
Black-throated Diver   *Gavia arctica* (L)
Slavonian Grebe   *Podiceps auritus* (L)
Red-necked Grebe   *Podiceps griseigena* (Boddaert)
Great Crested Grebe   *Podiceps cristatus* (L)
Gannet   *Sula bassana* (L)
Cormorant   *Phalacrocorax carbo* (L)
Heron   *Ardea cinerea* (L)
Bittern   *Botaurus stellaris* (L)
Glossy Ibis   *Plegadis falcinellus* (L)
Spoonbill   *Platalea leucorodia* (L)
Mute Swan   *Cygnus olor* (Gmelin)
Whooper Swan   *Cygnus cygnus* (L)
Bewick's Swan   *Cygnus bewickii* Yarrell
Black Swan   *Cygnus atratus* Latham
Pink-footed Goose   *Anser fabalis brachyrhynchus* Baillon
Forest Bean Goose   *Anser fabalis fabalis* (Latham)
Tundra Bean Goose   *Anser fabilis rossicus* Buturlin
Siberian White-fronted Goose   *Anser albifrons albifrons* (Scopoli)
Greenland White-fronted Goose   *Anser albifrons flavirostris* Dalgety and Scott
Western Greylag Goose   *Anser anser anser* (L)
Eastern Greylag Goose   *Anser anser rubrirostris* (Swinhoe)
Snow Goose   *Anser caerulescens (L)*
Canada Goose   *Branta canadensis* (L)
Barnacle Goose   *Branta leucopsis* (Bechstein)
Dark-breasted Brent Goose   *Branta bernicla bernicla* (L)
Light-breasted Brent Goose   *Branta bernicla hrota* (Müller)

GLOSSARY OF SCIENTIFIC NAMES

Pacific Brent Goose   *Branta bernicla nigricans* (Laurence)
Red-breasted Goose   *Branta ruficollis* (Pallas)
Ruddy Shelduck   *Tadorna ferruginea* (Pallas)
Shelduck   *Tadorna tadorna* (L)
Mandarin Duck   *Aix galericulata* (L)
Wigeon   *Anas penelope* (L)
American Wigeon   *Anas americana* Gmelin
Gadwall   *Anas strepera* L.
Teal   *Anas crecca* L.
Mallard   *Anas platyrhynchos* L.
Black Duck   *Anas rubrupes* Brewster
Pintail   *Anas acuta* L.
Garganey   *Anas querquedula* L.
Shoveler   *Anas clypeata* (L)
Red-crested Pochard   *Netta rufina* (Pallas)
Pochard   *Aythya ferina* (L)
Ferruginous Duck   *Aythya nyroca* (Güldenstadt)
Tufted Duck   *Aythya fuligula* (L)
Scaup   *Aythya marila* (L)
Eider   *Somateria mollissima* (L)
King Eider   *Somateria spectabilis* (L)
Long-tailed Duck   *Clangula hyemalis* (L)
Common Scoter   *Melanitta nigra* (L)
Surf Scoter   *Melanitta perspicillata* (L)
Velvet Scoter   *Melanitta fusca* (L)
Goldeneye   *Bucephala clangula* (L)
Smew   *Mergus albellus* L.
Red-breasted Merganser   *Mergus serrator* L.
Goosander   *Mergus merganser* L.
Marsh Harrier   *Circus aeruginosus* (L)
Montagu's Harrier   *Circus pygargus* (L)
Moorhen   *Gallinula chloropus* (L)
Coot   *Fulica atra* L.
Oystercatcher   *Haematopus ostralegus* L.
Lapwing   *Vanellus vanellus* (L)
Grey Plover   *Pluvialis squatarola* (L)
Golden Plover   *Pluvialis apricaria* (L)
Ringed Plover   *Charadrius hiaticula* L.
Little Ringed Plover   *Charadrius dubius* Scopoli
Kentish Plover   *Charadrius alexandrinus* L.
Dotterel   *Eudromias morinellus* (L)
Avocet   *Recurvirostra avosetta* L.
Whimbrel   *Numenius phaeopus* (L)
Curlew   *Numenius arquata* (L)
Black-tailed Godwit   *Limosa limosa* (L)
Bar-tailed Godwit   *Limosa lapponica* (L)
Spotted Redshank   *Tringa erythropus* (Pallas)

Redshank *Tringa totanus* (L)
Marsh Sandpiper *Tringa stagnatilis* (Bechstein)
Greenshank *Tringa nebularia* (Gunnerus)
Green Sandpiper *Tringa ochropus* L.
Solitary Sandpiper *Tringa solitaria* Wilson
Wood Sandpiper *Tringa glareola* L.
Common Sandpiper *Actitis hypoleucos* (L)
Turnstone *Arenaria interpres* (L)
Snipe *Gallinago gallinago* (L)
Jack Snipe *Lymnocryptes minima* (Brünnich)
Knot *Calidris canutus* (L)
Sanderling *Calidris alba* (Pallas)
Semi-palmated Sandpiper *Calidris pusillus* (L)
Western Sandpiper *Calidris mauri* (Cabanis)
Little Stint *Calidris minuta* (Leisler)
Temminck's Stint *Calidris temminckii* (Leisler)
Pectoral Sandpiper *Calidris melanotos* (Vieillot)
Purple Sandpiper *Calidris maritima* (Brünnich)
Dunlin *Calidris alpina* (L)
Curlew Sandpiper *Calidris ferruginea* (Pontoppidan)
Ruff *Philomachus pugnax* (L)
Arctic Skua *Stercorarius parasiticus* (L)
Common Gull *Larus canus* (L)
Herring Gull *Larus argentatus* Pontoppidan
Lesser Black-backed Gull *Larus fuscus* L.
Great Black-backed Gull *Larus marinus* L.
Glaucous Gull *Larus hyperboreus* Gunnerus
Mediterranean Gull *Larus melanocephalus* Temminck
Black-headed Gull *Larus ridibundus* L.
Little Gull *Larus minutus* Pallas
Kittiwake *Rissa tridactyla* (L)
Black Tern *Chlidonias niger* (L)
Common Tern *Sterna hirundo* L.
Arctic Tern *Sterna paradisaea* Pontoppidan
Little Tern *Sterna albifrons* Pallas
Sandwich Tern *Sterna sandvicensis* Latham
Partridge *Perdix perdix* (L)
Bearded Tit *Panurus biarmicus* (L)
Skylark *Alauda arvensis* L.
Meadow Pipit *Anthus pratensis* (L)
Yellow Wagtail *Motacilla flava flavissima* (Blyth)

PLANTS

Sea Couch Grass *Agropyron pungens*
Sea Meadow Grass *Puccinella maritima*
Red Fescue *Festuca rubra*

APPENDIX

Sea Barley   *Hordeum marinum*
Reflexed Saltmarsh Grass   *Puccinella distans*
Marsh Foxtail   *Alopecurus geniculatus*
Marsh Samphire   *Salicornia sp.*
Golden Samphire   *Inula crithmoides*
Sea Purslane   *Halimione portulacoides*
Hastate Orache   *Atriplex hastata*
Sea Aster   *Aster tripolium*
Sea Club Rush   *Scirpus maritimus*
Glaucous Club Rush   *Scirpus tabernaemontani*
Reed   *Phragmites communis*
Cord Grass   *Spartina maritima*
Cord Grass   *Spartina anglica*
Eel-Grass   *Zostera marina*
Eel-Grass   *Zostera noltii*
Sea Lettuce   *Enteropmorpha sp.*
Water Crowfoot   *Ranunculus aquatilis*
Milfoil   *Myriophyllum sp.*
Hornwort   *Ceratophyllum sp.*
Mare's Tail   *Hippuris vulgaris*
Spike-rush   *Eleocharis palustris*
Wheat   *Triticum sp.*
Barley   *Hordeum sp.*
Fennel-leaved Pondweed   *Potamogeton pectinatus*
Seablite   *Suaeda sp.*

INVERTEBRATES

Laver Spire Shell   *Hydrobia ulvae*
Common Mussel   *Mytilus edulis*
Shore Crab   *Carcinus maenus*
Shrimp   *Crangon vulgaris*
Ragworm   *Nereis sp.*

FISH

Dover Sole   *Solea solea*
Flounder   *Pleuronectes flesus*
Salmon   *Salmo salar*
Trout   *Salmo trutta*
Smelt   *Osmerus epirlanus*
Sand Goby   *Pomatoschistus minutus*
Sand Eel   *Amonolytes tobianus*
Lampern   *Lampetra fluviatilis*
Eel   *Anguilla anguilla*

MAMMAL

Brown Rat   *Rattus norvegicus*

BIBLIOGRAPHY

❧

ANDREWS, M. J. (1976) *The Occurrence of Tubificids in the Thames Estuary*, Thames Water Authority publication.

ANON (1973) *Notes on the Port of London*, Port of London Authority publication.

ANON (1974) *The Cleaner Thames – A Brief History of Pollution Control*, Port of London Authority leaflet.

ANON (1975) *Revised preliminary proposal for Maplin Seaport development*, Port of London Authority publication.

ANON (1975b) *Report on the predicted effect on the quality of the Thames Tideway of thermal discharges by established and proposed power stations*, Thames Water Authority publication.

ATKINSON-WILLES, G. (Ed.) (1963) *Wildfowl in Great Britain*, Monograph of the Nature Conservancy No. 3. H.M.S.O., London.

ATKINSON-WILLES, G. (in press) 'The numerical distribution of ducks, swans and coots as a guide in assessing the importance of wetlands.' *Proc. Int. Conf. Conserv. Wetlands and Waterfowl, Heiligenhaven 1974.*

BOYD, H., HARRISON, J. G. and ALLISON, A. (1975) *Duck Wings – a study of duck production*, WAGBI Con. Pub.

BURTON, J. F. (1958) 'The wildlife of London's last salt-marsh', *Kent and Sussex Journ. 3:445–447.*

BURTON, J. F. (1973) 'Duck and waders on the Thames, 1945–50', *Lond. Bird. Rep. 37:65–66.*

CHAPMAN, C. B. (1972) 'The year of the Great Stink', *The Pharos of Alpha Omega Alpha 35:90–105.*

CHARMAN, K. (in press) 'The Feeding Ecology of the Brent Goose', *Contract 205/2 for the research.* NERC *Report to Dept. of the Environment.*

CHURCHILL, A. (1933) 'Wigeon nesting in Kent', *Brit. Birds 26:275–276.*

COPELAND, W. O. (1967) 'Torrey Canyon Pollution', *Journ. Devon Trust Nat. Con. Supp. 8–11.*

COUNTRYSIDE COMMISSION (1970) *The Planning of the Coastline*, H.M.S.O., London.

ELLWOOD, J., HARRISON, J. G., MOULAND, H. and RUXTON, J. (1971) 'Greylag Geese in South-east England', WAGBI *Ann. Rep. 1970–71:61–62.*

GEORGE, R. W. (1973) 'Birds at Surrey Commercial Docks, April 1971 to December 1972', *Lond. Bird Rep. 37:67–70.*

GILLHAM, E. H. and HOMES, R. C. (1950) *The Birds of the North Kent Marshes*, Collins, London.

GILLHAM, E. H. and HARRISON, J. G. (1963) 'Kent' in *Wildfowl in Great Britain: 70–76.* Nature Conservancy Monograph. H.M.S.O.

GLEGG, W. E. (1929) *A History of the Birds of Essex*, Witherby, London.

BIBLIOGRAPHY

GRANT, P. J. (1970) 'Duck on the River Thames at Woolwich', *Lond. Bird Rep.* *34:80–85.*

GRANT, P. J. (1971) 'Birds at Surrey Commercial Docks', *Lond. Bird Rep.* *35:87–91.*

GRANT, P. J., HARRISON, J. G. and NOBLE, K. (1973) 'The return of birdlife to the Inner Thames', *Lond. Bird. Rep. 37:61–64.*

GRANT, P. J., SWIFT, J. and HARRISON, J. G. (1973) 'The return of Wildfowl to the Inner Thames', *WAGBI Ann. Rep. 1972–73:44–52.*

GREENHALGH, M. (1975) *The Wildfowl of the Ribble Estuary*, WAGBI Cons. Pub.

HARRISON, J. G. (1952) *Estuary Saga*, Witherby, London.

HARRISON, J. G. (1954) *Pastures New*, Witherby, London.

HARRISON, J. G. (1970) 'The Breeding Birds of Chetney', *Kent Orn. Soc. Special Supplement.*

HARRISON, J. G. (1971a) 'MIDA and the Medway Estuary', *WAGBI Ann. Rep. 1970–71:74–76.*

HARRISON, J. G. (1971b) 'Medway Estuary Crisis', *World of Birds 1:4:4–7.*

HARRISON, J. G. (1972a) 'The Medway Estuary – a threatened wetland of international importance', *WAGBI Ann. Rep. 1971–72:66–68.*

HARRISON, J. G. (1972b) *Wildfowl of the North Kent Marshes*, WAGBI Cons. Pub.

HARRISON, J. G. (1975) *Kingsnorth Power Station Wildfowl Reserve*, CEGB Publication.

HARRISON, J. G. and BUCK, W. F. A. (1967) *Peril in Perspective*, Kent Orn. Soc. Special Supplement.

HARRISON, J. G. and BUCK, W. F. A. (1968) 'Immigrant Mute Swans in Kent', *Kent Bird Rep. 16:83–84.*

HARRISON, J. G., GRANT, P. J. and SWIFT, J. (1976 in press) 'Thames Transformed', *Proc. Int. Conf. Conserv. Wetlands and Waterfowl, Heiligenhaven 1974.*

HARRISON, J. G. and HUDSON, M. (1964) 'Some effects of severe weather on wildfowl in Kent', *Wildfowl Trust 15th Ann. Rep. 26–32.*

HARRISON, J. G., HUMPHREYS, J. N. and GRAVES, G. (1972) *Breeding Birds of the Medway Estuary*, WAGBI Con. Pub. jointly with the Kent Orn. Soc.

HARRISON, J. G. and McLEAN, A. (1947) 'The effect of severe weather on Wigeon', *Brit. Birds 40:218.*

HARRISON, J. G. and OGILVIE, M. (1967) 'Immigrant Mute Swans in South-east England', *Wildfowl Trust 18th Ann. Rep. 85–87.*

HARRISON, J. M. (1953) *The Birds of Kent*, Witherby, London.

HARRISON, J. M. and HARRISON, J. G. (1970 'Mid-summer movements of duck in South-east England', *WAGBI Ann. Rep. 1969–70:64–68.*

HARRISON, J. M., HARRISON, J. G. and HARRISON, D. L. (1969) 'Some preliminary results from the release of hand-reared Gadwall', *WAGBI Ann. Rep. 1968–69:37–40.*

HARRISON, J. M., HARRISON, J. G. and HUDSON, M. (1967) 'Melanistic White-fronted and other Geese', *Wildfowl Trust 18th Ann. Rep. 153–155.*

HORI, J. (1966) 'Observations on Pochard and Tufted Duck breeding biology with particular reference to colonisation of home range', *Bird Study: 13:297–305.*

BIBLIOGRAPHY

HORN, P. W. (1921) 'The birds of West Thurrock Marsh', *Essex Nat.* 19:262–266.

HUDSON, M. J. (1967) 'The breeding wildfowl of the North Kent Marshes, 1961–64', *Kent Bird Rep.* 15:85–98.

HUDSON, R. and PYMAN, G. A. (1968) *A Guide to the Birds of Essex*, Clarke, London and Chelmsford.

INTERNATIONAL UNION FOR THE CONSERVATION OF NATURE AND NATURAL RESOURCES (1965) *List of European and North African Wetlands of International Importance* IUCN, Morges.

KAY, D. G. and KNIGHTS, R. D. (1975) 'The Macro-invertebrate Fauna of the Intertidal Soft Sediments of South-east England', *Journal Mar. Bio. Ass. UK:* 55:811–832.

KENT ORNITHOLOGICAL SOCIETY (1952–73) *Kent Bird Report: 1–22.*

KENT COUNTY COUNCIL (1970) 'The Potential of the Medway Estuary as a Maritime Industrial Development Area', Maidstone.

LONDON NATURAL HISTORY SOCIETY (1964) *The Birds of the London Area*, Hart-Davis, London.

LONDON NATURAL HISTORY SOCIETY (1936–73) *London Bird Report: 1–35.*

LIPPENS, L. (1971) 'Reintroducing the Greylag in Belgium', *WAGBI Ann. Rep.* 1970–71:62–66.

MAXWELL, C. and BAKER, A. (1967) 'Oil and Detergent Pollution', *Journ. Devon Trust Nat. Con. Supp.:* 39–72.

MEDWAY PRESERVATION SOCIETY (1971) *The Effects of a Maritime Industrial Development Area on the Medway Estuary.*

MOULAND, W., MOULAND, H. and HARRISON, J. G. (1970) 'The Netherby Experiment repeated with Teal', *WAGBI Ann. Rep.* 1969–70: 55–56.

NATURE CONSERVANCY (1971) *Wildlife Conservation in the North Kent Marshes,* Report of a Working party.

NATURE CONSERVANCY COUNCIL (1974) *A Habitat Assessment of the Foulness area.*

NOBLE, K. (1971a) 'Birds of Rainham Marsh', *Lond. Bird. Rep.:* 35:56–68.

NOBLE, K. (1971b) 'Seabird watching on the River Thames', *Lond. Bird Rep.:* 35:92.

NOBLE, K. (1972) 'Oystercatchers breeding at Rainham Marsh, Essex', *Lond. Bird Rep.:* 36:91.

OGILVIE, M. A. (1962) 'The movements of Shoveler ringed in Britain', *Wildfowl Trust 13th Ann. Rep.:* 65–69.

OGILVIE, M. A. and MATTHEWS, G. V. T. (1969) 'Brent Geese, Mudflats and Man', *Wildfowl 20:119–125.*

OLIVER, P. J. (1974) 'Heronries in the London Area', *Lond. Bird Rep.:* 38:73–77.

OLNEY, P. (1963) 'The food & feeding habits of Teal, *Anas crecca crecca.'* *Proc. Zool. Soc. London: 140: 397–418.*

OLNEY, P. (1965a) 'The food and feeding habits of Shelduck *Tadorna tadorna*', *Ibis: 107:527–532.*

OLNEY, P. (1965b) 'The autumn and winter feeding biology of certain sympatric ducks', *Trans. 5th Cong. Int. Union Game Biol.:* 309–320.

OLNEY, P. (1970) 'Food habits of wildfowl in Great Britain', *The New Wildfowler in the 1970's:* 86–97: Barrie and Jenkins, London.

234

BIBLIOGRAPHY

PARSLOW, J. L. F. (1967) 'Changes in status among breeding birds in Britain and Ireland', *Brit. Birds: 60:2–47 et seq.*

PITHERS, E. (1971) 'Estimated breeding populations – the Thames', *Wildfowl Cons. in North Kent Marshes:* Appendix.

POTTER, J. H. (1971a) 'Pollution Control and the Port of London', *Port of London: 46:3–7.*

POTTER, J. H. (1971b) 'Pollution and its control in the Tidal Thames', *Community Health: 3:103–110.*

PRATER, A. (1971) *Birds of Estuaries Enquiry – Report on the Pilot Survey* and subsequent reports. Joint B.T.O./R.S.P.B. Publication.

PRENTIS, W. (1894) *Birds of Rainham*, London.

SALOMONSEN, F. (1958) 'The Present Status of the Brent Goose in Western Europe', *Vidensk Medd. Dansk. Naturh. Foren. 120:43–80.*

SMITH, D. J., NICHOLSON, R. A. and MOORE, P. J. (1971) 'Mercury in the Water of the Tidal Thames', *Nature 232:393–394.*

'SON OF THE MARSHES' (1895) *Annals of a Fishing Village*, London.

ST JOSEPH, A. and BENNETT, T. J. (in press) 'A study of the movements of Brent Geese', NERC *Report to Dept. of the Environment. Contract 205/2 for the research.*

STRANGEMAN, P. J. (1971) 'Birds of the River Thames at Westminster, 1968–1970', *Lond. Bird Rep.: 35:73–80.*

TETLOW, A. (1972) 'Towards a Cleaner River', *Port of London: 47:12–13.*

TICEHURST, N. (1909) *The Birds of Kent*, Witherby, London.

TRUESDALE, G. A. (1975) 'European Environment Problems and Solutions in Water Pollution', *Water Pollution Control 74:11–17.*

WALPOLE-BOND, J. (1909) 'Pochard nesting in north Kent', *Brit. Birds: 2:383–384.*

WHEELER, A. (1970) 'Fish return to the Thames', *Science Journal, November, 1970: 28–32.*

WHEELER, A. (1971) 'Thames Trout and other fishes', *Port of London: 46:163–165.*

WHITLOCK, R. (Ed.) (1934–47) *South-Eastern Bird Reports.*

WILDFOWL TRUST (1974–75) *Brent Goose Research Newsletters 1–3 Limited Circulation.*

WOOD, L. B. (1971) 'The Cleaner Thames', GLC *Intelligence Unit Quarterly Bull.: 17:37–48.*

WOOD, L. B. (1973) 'The Condition of London's River in 1971', GLC *Intelligence Unit Quarterly Bulletin 22:18–35.*

WYER, DR. D. W. and WATERS, R. (in press) 'The Tidal Flat Zostera and Algal Vegetation', NERC *Report to Dept. of the Environment. Contract 205/2 for the research.*

YARKER, B. and ATKINSON-WILLES, G. (1971) 'The numerical distribution of some British breeding ducks', *Wildfowl: 22:63–70.*

INDEX

❧

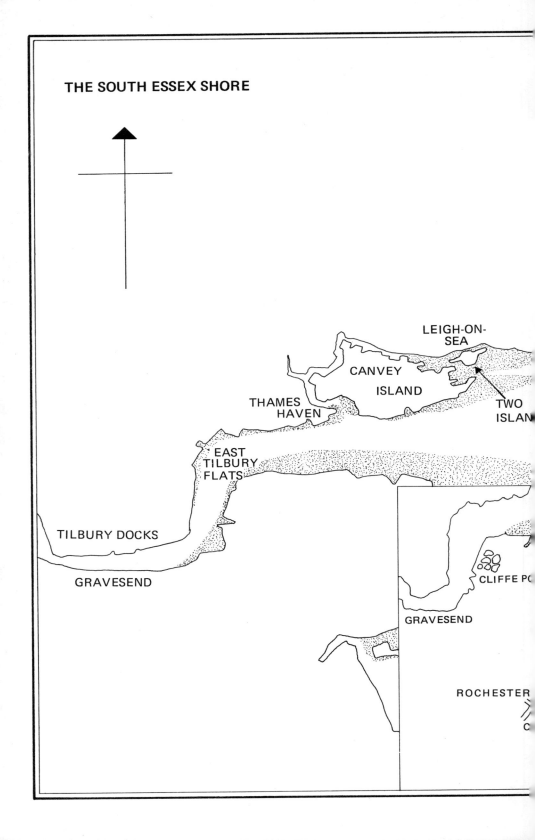

THE SOUTH ESSEX SHORE

LEIGH-ON-SEA

CANVEY ISLAND

THAMES HAVEN

TWO ISLAN

EAST TILBURY FLATS

TILBURY DOCKS

GRAVESEND

CLIFFE PO

GRAVESEND

ROCHESTER